DIALECT

DIVERSITY

IN AMERICA

D I A L

**The
Politics
of Language
Change**

D I V E

I N A M

WILLIAM LABOV

E   C   T

R   S   I   T   Y

E   R   I   C   A

PAGE-BARBOUR LECTURES FOR 2009

University of Virginia Press   *Charlottesville and London*

University of Virginia Press
© 2012 by the Rector and Visitors of the University of Virginia
All rights reserved
Printed in the United States of America on acid-free paper

First published 2012
First paperback edition published 2014
ISBN 978-0-8139-3588-1 (paper)

9 8 7 6 5 4 3 2 1

The Library of Congress has cataloged the hardcover edition as follows:

LIBRARY OF CONGRESS CATALOGING-IN-PUBLICATION DATA
Labov, William.
    Dialect diversity in America : the politics of language change / William Labov.
        p.   cm.—(Page-Barbour lectures)
    Includes bibliographical references and index.
    ISBN 978-0-8139-3326-9 (cloth : alk. paper)—ISBN 978-0-8139-3327-6 (e-book)
    1. English language—Dialects—United States. 2. English language—Variation—
United States. 3. English language—Social aspects—United States. 4. English
language—Political aspects—United States. 5. Linguistic change—United States.
6. African Americans—Languages. 7. Black English. 8. Sociolinguistics. I. Title.
    PE2841.L33 2012
    427'.973—dc23

                                                                    2012009828

Contents

Preface   vii

1. About Language and Language Change   1

2. A Hidden Consensus   9

3. Hidden Diversity   17

4. The Growing Divergence of Black and White English   38

5. The Politics of African American English   68

6. Language Change as Local Politics   98

7. The Political Ideology of the Northern Cities Shift   109

8. Putting It All Together   135

Appendix: Summary Statement on African
    American Vernacular English   141

Notes   151

References   157

Index   165

Preface

When Eve Danziger invited me to give the 2009 Page-Barbour lectures, I was embarrassed as much as honored. I found that my predecessors in this series included those who had influenced me most deeply in the unlimited ambition of my early years. The list is so long that it would be claiming too much to name them here. But thinking of what I might say, I could only imagine an audience of these lecturers and of what I have to offer them. Now that my efforts to understand the world had focused on language and language change, how could I demonstrate that in the fifty years since I had read what they had to say, I had not wasted my time?

I was not worried about capturing the interest of the audience. Whenever I show that the dialects of American English are becoming more different from each other over time, the finding is so contrary to expectation that the audience demands an explanation. It is not only a challenge to our appreciation of the power of the mass media to control our behavior, but more profoundly, a challenge to our understanding of language as a means of communication. Even further, it puts into question our confidence in the rationality of human nature.

Any such accounting must also overcome the problem of communication between the linguist and the public at large. In no other form of human behavior is there such a great gap between reality and public discussion of it. Most of the sound changes I will discuss are inaudible and unknown to those affected by them. When language changes do rise to the level of social awareness, the stereotypes used to stigmatize them have only marginal relation to what is actually said in everyday speech. As a result, the field linguist interested in these changing patterns cannot focus overtly on the object of interest, since most people will reject the new forms once they become aware of them. In many areas of culture or technology, some older people will embrace and welcome the new. But in thousands of sociolinguistic interviews, no one has ever been heard to say, "I really like the way that young people talk today; it's so much better than the way we talked when I was young." Most of us adhere to what one may call the Golden Age Syndrome: the belief that language once existed in a state of perfection, and any change is a decline from that state, to be resisted.

Much of the dialect diversity in America is the result of the growing divide between mainstream white dialects and African American Vernacular English (AAVE). Here the problem of communication is even deeper, and much of this book will be devoted to showing that the speech of African Americans is a coherent, well-formed, and different system, a fact obvious to all linguists but not at all to the general public. People who cannot detect a shred of racial bias in their own thinking will be profoundly biased in their reactions to African American speech. The ways in which race affects our views of language will intersect with our general effort to appreciate the role of rationality in linguistic matters.

I hope that my efforts to cross the gap between linguistic description and general literacy will lay the foundation for this effort to identify the driving forces in linguistic change. This foundation is only a first step, since the larger social forces plainly call for an interdisciplinary accounting. My own work on language stratification and language change is relevant to academic groups in fields beyond linguistics, as is evident from the fact that this invitation comes from a distinguished anthropologist. I have had fruitful interactions with many areas of psychology and sociology. These lectures reach out to historians and political scientists as well, areas in which my competence is more limited, even accidental. The word politics in the subtitle is indeed a central theme of the work, and we will see that the issues to be discussed are highly politicized. The argument will conclude with an effort to account for the striking coincidence between the Blue States of the 2004–8 elections and the major example of dialect divergence: the Northern Cities Shift.

Turning then to my imaginary audience of predecessors, I hope to persuade them that there is some profit in studying the instability of English, the means of communication that they used in their lectures, and that an explanation lies in the political nature of the animal that uses it.

Among my many intellectual debts that might be mentioned here, I will cite only one, to my colleague and wife, Gillian Sankoff, who has pondered these matters with me over three decades, and corrected innumerable errors of fact and logic in these lectures.

DIALECT

DIVERSITY

IN AMERICA

1 ⟷ ABOUT LANGUAGE AND LANGUAGE CHANGE

This book is about language, about language change in particular, and especially about the changes that are now taking place in the dialects of North American English. It is also about the political causes and consequences of those changes. What is said here about language and linguistic change has a firm foundation in four decades of research on American English. On the other hand, I am not an expert in politics. For this area, I have drawn from the work of a wide range of historians, political scientists, and cultural geographers to make the necessary connections.

Some Commonsense Views of Language That Are Wrong

People tend to believe that dialect differences in American English are disappearing, especially given our exposure to a fairly uniform broadcast standard in the mass media. One can find this point of view in almost any discussion of American dialects, as for example in a recent exchange on *Dr. Goodword's Language Blog.*[1] A contributor, Bruce, wrote:

> The accents I do hear from people from around the country seem to be disappearing. People from New Orleans interviewed on TV or Radio seem to sound like me, as do many of those I hear from New York and elsewhere. I used to hear distinctive accents from people from Minnesota for example and those also seem to be going.

Dr. Goodword responded:

Bruce is absolutely right. Regional accents are dying out . . . the original dialects in this country were the results of the accents of the various immigrants who came to this country looking for a better life. They all landed on the east coast, which is why all the accents are currently in the east. However, as they migrated to the west, all these accents merged into one, so there are no distinctive regional dialects west or north of southern Ohio (maybe southern Illinois and a bit in northern Minnesota).

This overwhelmingly common opinion is simply and jarringly wrong. The research reported here will demonstrate that the reverse is actually the case. New sound changes in progress are driving the regional dialects of English further and further apart, so that people from Los Angeles, Chicago, Toronto, Philadelphia, and New York speak more differently from each other now than they did in the middle of the 20th century. I would not expect most readers of this book to accept this statement lightly, and I will do my best to put enough evidence before you to make it believable. We will be dealing with sounds that are not easy to describe in print, but I will try to direct your hearing so that you can begin to observe some of these new sound changes around you in everyday life.

This book is a product of sociolinguistic research, in which we interview people in communities across the country and record conversation that comes as close as possible to the speech of everyday life. This approach produces surprising results that often run counter to preconceived intuitions and opinions. The growing divergence of dialects is only one case where our findings are contrary to accepted opinion. It will also appear, in spite of public perception, that there is no such thing as "Brooklynese" (chap. 3). Chapter 4 will demonstrate that popular descriptions of "Ebonics" bear little relation to what African American people actually say.

What We All Know about Language and What We Don't Know

In the chapters to follow, I assume no knowledge of linguistics, though many readers will be quite at home in that field. Even without any knowledge of linguistics, your own knowledge of language will be an important resource in the discussion to come. Most linguists begin their introductory classes by saying, "You already know more about your language than any other subject you will ever study." You may not know that you know this, since most linguistic knowledge is implicit, hidden from conscious view. Most of what linguists do is to make that knowledge explicit, asking direct questions such as "Can you say *Service is bad around here anymore?*," or more commonly asking themselves, "Can I say *Service is bad around here anymore?*" This is a useful and productive procedure, and most progress in linguistic theory is built upon it. Yet other aspects of language are hidden from these introspective procedures, and can only be found by observation of what people say. This is the case for many kinds of linguistic variation.

The main topic of chapter 2 is such a case of variation, taken as an example of the uniform way in which our language shifts and changes from one time to another. It is the alternation between *Good morning* and *Good mornin'*.[2] Some features of this variation are open to introspection. As a native speaker of English, I know that I can say either *Morning* or *mornin'*. And if I ask myself, "Can I say *Flushin', Long Island?*, the answer is accurately "No." The results of observation confirm this: no one has been heard to say *Flushin', Long Island*. On the other hand, introspection fails if I ask myself whether I am more likely to use the *-in'* variant in *Good morning* or in *I'm working on it*. Here the answer would probably be, "It all depends; both are possible." Yet all studies of what people actually say find that the *-in'* form is much more likely in progressive verbs like *workin'* than in nouns like *morning* and *ceiling* (Labov 1989; Houston 1991; Roberts 1993). And if I ask, "Is Sarah Palin more likely to say *Good mornin'* than Barack Obama?," most people will answer, "Yes." But as we will see, that answer is incorrect. It turns out that most of our introspective judgments about language are right, but a small percentage are dead wrong. The problem is that we don't have a clue as to where those errors are located. The data that will be used throughout this book will therefore be drawn from sociolinguistic studies that don't have that kind of uncertainty. They draw upon recorded sociolinguistic interviews that last an hour or more. These interviews are not like survey questionnaires. Rather, they are shaped like conversation, often touch on personal topics of great importance, and approximate—

but never quite reach—the style that people use in speaking to their friends and family in everyday life. Because actual behavior is variable in the items we are interested in, this requires the systematic study of variation—how individual speakers vary from one style to another, and how speakers' language patterns vary from one social group to another.[3]

The Two Main Strategies of Linguistic Research

Among the paths that linguists follow in pursuit of a better understanding of human language, we can trace two main branches.

THE SEARCH FOR UNIVERSAL GRAMMAR. One way of understanding language follows a search for the features that are common to all languages, a "universal grammar."[4] This is the goal set for linguistics by Noam Chomsky (1968). However this common human language faculty may have originated, it must have remained constant during all of human history. We know this by the fact that children of any genetic subgroup can learn any language as their first language equally well. By definition, this universal grammar has a null footprint in time.

UNDERSTANDING LANGUAGE CHANGE. The other route toward a greater understanding of language focuses on linguistic change. We ask how the great differentiation of language families, languages, and dialects came about. We would like to know how any given language or dialect came to be, and more generally, what are the root causes of language change and diversity? The subject matter of this study is quite large: every aspect of language that is changing or has changed in the past. Historical linguistics attacks the problem through the written record of past changes; in recent years, the study of linguistic change and variation has focused on changes taking place around us, changes still in progress.

The study of language change will tell us about ourselves, what kind of people are we, and how we have evolved. Darwin was well aware of this. In the *Descent of Man* (1871) he famously wrote that "the formation of different languages and of distinct species, and the proofs that both have been developed through a gradual process, are curiously parallel." He then laid out 15 such parallels having to do with the effects of long continued use, such as:

- We find in distinct languages striking homologies due to communities of descent,
- and analogies due to a similar process of formation.
- Dominant languages and dialects spread widely
- and lead to the gradual extinction of other tongues.
- We see variability in every tongue, and new words are continually cropping up; . . .
- single words, like whole languages, gradually become extinct.

But when Darwin came to the crucial question of natural selection, he had to argue,

- The survival or preservation of certain favoured words in the struggle for existence is natural selection.

As much we admire and follow Darwin, no linguist supports this view. The general consensus is that there is no progress in linguistic evolution. Writing on "language and evolution," Joseph Greenberg summed up the consensus:

Taking linguistic change as a whole, there seems to be no discernible movement toward greater efficiency such as might be expected if in fact there were a continuous struggle in which superior linguistic innovations won out as a general rule. (1959)

The parallels between linguistic and biological evolution seem so strong that it is indeed puzzling to find that the crucial link of natural selection should be missing. Language change across the centuries has turned a single group of Proto-Indo-European dialects into a family of mutually unintelligible languages, including Russian, Hindi, Greek, Albanian, French, German, English, and Icelandic. Linguistic change has not made it easier for speakers of those languages to communicate.

Before we begin a search for the causes of language change and diversity, it should be said that the mere fact of diversity is not a challenge to our understanding. When two groups of speakers become separated over time by migration to distant parts, and communication between them is drastically reduced, we expect their linguistic systems to diverge. The many sources of variation in vocabulary, grammar, and phonology will inevitably lead them to drift apart, and any degree of convergence requires an explanation.

On the other hand, we are not surprised when neighboring dialects converge. Many studies of European dialects show how the dialect contact leads to reduction of dialect diversity in the form of "dialect leveling" (Trudgill 1986). In fact, if these neighbors begin to speak more differently from one another, we are surprised and puzzled. It follows that when two speech communities are in continuous communication, linguistic convergence is expected and any degree of divergence requires an explanation.

Is Language a Property of the Individual or the Group?

This bears on our most general view of what the language faculty is and how it varies. Many linguists believe that language is a property of the individual mind, and it is only natural for each individual to have constructed a different language of their own. The sociolinguistic view, which guides my own thinking, is that we are programmed to learn to speak in ways that fit the general pattern of our community. What I, as a language learner, want to learn is not "my English" or even "your English" but the English language in general. In this sense, the language learning faculty is *outward bound*, searching for a community consensus rather than an individual model.

We can easily imagine a different scenario of linguistic evolution. If the language learner was fixed on the first linguistic pattern encountered, the language of the parent, we would expect that when families move into a new area, children would grow up using their parents' dialect. Yet we have massive evidence that children do not do this: if they are brought into a new community before the age of nine, children will have the dialect system of that community, not of their parents. It appears that linguistic evolution has developed a system that searches for the general pattern of the speech community and, up to a certain age, continually rewrites the rules as it encounters new data.

If this search for what is "out there" is the driving force in language acquisition, we have to ask, what happens when the language learner finds no single pattern but variation in the way that people speak? To answer this question, the chapters to follow will consider a number of such "linguistic variables," and speakers' ways of dealing with them.

The Argument to Follow

Chapter 2 begins with the most general patterns—what we all know but don't know we know about linguistic variation. We will see that the linguistic variation of big cities like New York is surprisingly regular across social groups and social situations. We will find a strong social consensus in how we change our way of speaking from one situation to another, and consider experimental evidence on how powerful that hidden consensus is. Chapter 3 will turn to the disruption of that consensus and describe the sound changes that drive dialects apart—in particular, the Northern Cities Shift, which rotates the short vowels of cities in the Great Lakes region. It will appear that such regional changes interfere with our ability to understand one another, not only when we travel, but within the very community in which we were born and raised.

Chapter 4 pursues even larger language differences, confronting the growing gulf between white and black forms of English. We will look into the origins of this division and find that African American Vernacular English is not a direct descendant of the English spoken by slaves on southern plantations, as we used to think. Its present form is rather a new development fostered by residential segregation in the great cities of the North, and spread in complex and mysterious ways throughout the country as a whole.

Chapter 5 deals with the consequences of the growing divergence in Black and White English. The immediate cause of this widening gap is the residential segregation characteristic of all the major cities of the United States. In addition to fostering dialect differences between black and white Americans, residential segregation also has severe effects on African American literacy. The history of reactions to the use of different dialects of English in the classroom is a violent one, and the chapter ends by outlining some methods developed for teaching reading that take these linguistic and political factors into account.

Chapter 6 returns to the general study of dialect divergence and examines dialect as an emblem of local identity. The strengths and weaknesses of this account will be brought forward as the focus moves from neighborhoods to cities to metropolitan regions. It will appear that, in ways not yet understood, the mainstream dialect of the metropolis is geographically uniform. The widely used term "Brooklynese" turns out to be a label for working-class New York City speech, no matter where in the five boroughs the speakers may be living.

Chapter 7 examines the history of the Northern Cities Shift and the relation between linguistic change and political ideology over vast territories and several centuries. We will not leave race behind, for it will appear that attitudes toward race and racial inequality are deeply embedded in that history. The inquiry will carry us back to the construction of the Erie Canal in 1817, the great religious awakening of the 1820s and '30s, the formation of the Republican Party and the Civil War, and then carry us forward to the Civil Rights Act of 1964, the geographic reversal of Democratic and Republican territories, and the striking coincidence of the Northern dialect and the so-called Blue States of 2004 and 2008. The parallels between political and linguistic change show how intimately connected are these two forms of social behavior.

2 ↔ A HIDDEN CONSENSUS

Chapter 1 looked briefly at the difference between *-ing* and *-in'* in unstressed syllables at the ends of words; the difference between *He is working* and *He is workin'*, or between *Good morning* and *Good mornin'*. Speakers of English have alternated between these two forms for over a thousand years. The *-in'* form is the regular descendant of the Old English participle ending in *-inde*, and the *-ing* form is inherited from the Old English verbal noun ending in *-inge*. This alternation is a classic example of a *linguistic variable*, labeled (ING).

The (ING) Variable

This linguistic feature was first examined quantitatively by the anthropologist John Fischer in a 1958 study of 15 children in a New England town. Fischer found that boys used more *-in'* than girls, that a "typical boy" used more than a "model boy," and that children used much more *-in'* in informal speech than they did in the Thematic Apperception Test. I used the (ING) variable, among others, to study the social stratification of English in New York City in 1966.[1] This was the first systematic study of how speech varied systematically across social classes, ethnic groups, age groups. Before that time, descriptions of New York City speech concluded that it was "chaotic," that the variation from speaker to speaker and moment to moment was unpredictable.

(ING) on the Lower East Side of New York City

Figure 1 is drawn from interviews in that first random survey of the Lower East Side of New York City. The vertical axis is the percentage of the -*in'* variant out of all occurrences of (ING) in running speech.[2] The horizontal axis registers three different styles of speech. On the left is *casual speech*, typically drawn from narratives of vital events in the speaker's life, which approaches the speech of everyday life; *careful speech* is the bulk of the interview style; at right, the *reading* of particular words yields a view of the style in which the most attention is given to speech. Each of the lines connects the mean values for a given socioeconomic group: lower working class, upper working class, lower middle class, and upper middle class.

This regular pattern shows two independent effects, which tell us two different things about the speech community. For each style, we see social differentiation in the use of (ING): the lower the social class, the more -*in'*. At the same time, all New Yorkers *agree* in their evaluation of this variable. All social class groups decrease their use of -*in'* with increasing attention paid to speech. This display of the regularity of the effects of style and social class contributed to a change in the general linguistic view of the urban speech community. Variation of this type is now seen as "orderly heterogeneity," a new paradigm that defines a "speech community." In the constant slope of style shifting, we see a community united by consensus, yet in each context differentiated by social class. Patterns like this have since been found in hundreds of other cities and other languages.[3] The study of such stable sociolinguistic variables has yielded rich information on the sharpness of social stratification in a given community. Those communities that show steeper slopes of style shifting reflect a consciousness of social norms that is associated with strong upward social mobility (Labov 1966a). Social awareness of this pattern is acquired early in life; we have since learned that children acquire such style shifting of (ING) between three and four years of age (Roberts 1997).

The Social Perception of (ING)

Recently we asked whether the fine-grained differences in speech production seen in figure 1 correspond to what people can actually perceive as they listen to others speak. We carried out an experiment (Labov et al. 2011) to see whether listeners notice differences as small as 10% in the use -*in'* vs. -*ing*. We prepared seven different versions of

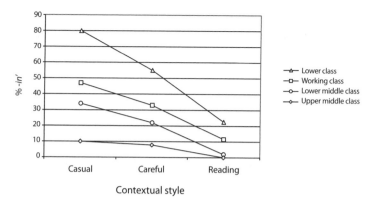

FIGURE 1. Stylistic and social stratification of the variable (ING) in New York City (from Labov 1966b).

a news broadcast with ten sentences, each containing one verb with -ing. In these different versions, the speaker used the informal -in' in varying proportions: 0%, 10%, 20%, 30%, 50%, 70%, and 100% of the sentences. (Our speakers actually read the broadcast with all -ing and all -in', and we spliced the words together in the different proportions.) Our subjects were told, "A young woman from Philadelphia has been studying to be a newscaster, and has applied for a job with a local radio station. Here are seven versions of a trial newscast that she read to submit with her job application."

Here are the first two sentences as heard in Trial 1 with -ing in the first sentence and -in' in the second:

- President Bush announced tonight that he was *putting* all available White House resources into support for the new tax cut bill.
- Democratic leaders of the House and Senate are *preparin'* compromise legislation.

After listening to all ten sentences for a given trial, subjects were asked to put a check mark in one of seven boxes in a scale like this:

Perfectly professional   Try another line of work

    1   2   3   4   5   6   7

/ ——— / ——— / —— / ——— / ——— / ——— / ——— /

The results followed a remarkably consistent pattern, not only in Philadelphia, but in other regions of the country as well. Figure 2 shows the result for a group of 36 college-student judges. The vertical axis is the mean ratings, running from "Perfectly professional" at the bottom to "Try another line of work" at the top, so the lower the score, the better the rating. The horizontal axis shows 0%, 10%, 20%, 30%, 50%, 70%, and 100% -*in'*. There are two main findings that we draw from this figure. The first is obvious. People agree that the -*in'* form is not appropriate for a news broadcaster, and they are sensitive to the use of -*in'* and -*ing* in a way that we would predict, being members of the same speech community: when listeners hear more -*in'*, they rate the speakers lower in their capacity to be broadcasters.

The second result is not so obvious: responses follow a declining curve as percentage of -*in'* increases. It is in fact a very specific curve, a logarithmic pattern. The R^2 figure of .97 means that the data fit this pattern very well: it accounts for 97% of the variation in the responses. This means that the impression created on the listener by an -*in'* pronunciation is proportional to the number he or she has already heard. To put it another way, listeners hear -*ing* as the norm for a news announcer, and -*in'* is a deviation from that norm. The effect of each deviation is not the same, rather it is proportional to the increase in the percentage of deviations from the expected norm. Thus listeners rate a perfect performance with 0% -*in'* at 18 on the scale, close to "Professional"; when they hear a single -*in'*, their rating jumps to 32, almost double. When they hear a second -*in'*, they raise the mean score only 6 points, from 32 to 38. And when the percent -*in'* rises from 70% to 100%, listeners raise the rating increase only 9%, 4 points on the rating scale.

Extending the Experiment to South Carolina

We wanted to know whether this pattern was the same for speakers of different dialects of English, and so carried out experiments in other sections of the country. The experiment was repeated with undergraduates at the University of South Carolina. There we found that listeners responded with a somewhat flatter curve—they were critical of the use of -*in'* for newscasting, but less so. We then recorded a USC faculty member reading the same passage. His strong southern

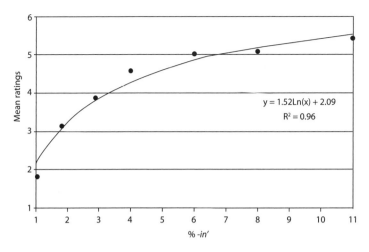

FIGURE 2. Philadelphia listeners' responses to Experiment 1 on sensitivity to frequency of -in' and -ing.

accent was radically different from that of the speaker of the Philadelphia experiment, who was a conservative representative of the Chicago dialect. Though there are many other variables that might affect the ratings of the two speakers by the South Carolina listeners, the experiment extracts the identical curve of responses and the same high fit of the data to the logarithmic model. The R^2 correlations of .98 for the Chicago speaker and .96 for the South Carolina speaker both show a very close fit to the logarithmic curve. The South Carolina listeners behave in the same way as the Philadelphia listeners, no matter who they are listening to. They agree that professional news broadcasters should not say *preparin'* but stay close to the standard model of *preparing*, and they react in the same way: the effect of each deviation from the norm is proportional to the increase in deviations.

The Political Use of (ING)

We are all constrained by this social consensus, even presidents. Figure 3 shows the use of -in' and -ing by President Obama. I was able to observe a sample of his casual speech in a recording made at a Father's Day barbeque on the White House lawn. The president donned an apron and chatted with the well-known chef Bobby Flay as he picked up tips on good barbeque technique.[4] The left-hand value

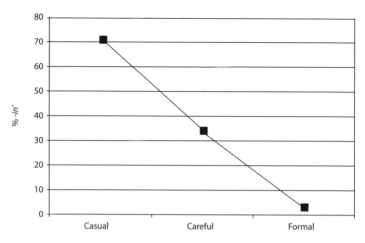

FIGURE 3. President Obama's use of (ING) in three contextual styles.

on figure 3 registers an *-in'* percentage of 72% for this occasion. Next is the president's more careful speech at the Father's Day ceremonies that followed, asking and answering political questions. His percentage of *-in'* falls to 33%. The most formal context shown is his scripted acceptance speech at the Democratic National Convention, where we see only 3% *-in'*.

One might think that some individuals might defy this convention to establish their own brand of colloquial style. In fact, the Republican vice presidential candidate, Sarah Palin, was widely criticized for what was seen as her idiosyncratic use of *-in'* in public speaking:

> When you speak in public, you use your best English, except for occasional emphases. Adopting Palin's de-G-ed "speakin'" is an assault on the language, just like perpetrating the lie that she's ready to lead is an assault on the future of the nation. (Rob Kall, on radio station WNJC)

However, if we take the same objective measures of the variable (ING), we find no difference between Sarah Palin and President Obama. For careful speech, we can take Sarah Palin's interviews with Katie Couric, and for scripted formal style, her acceptance speech at the Republican National Convention. Figure 4 superimposes the figures for Sarah Palin on those for President Obama. One could not obtain a more complete agreement. It is evident that Sarah Palin is

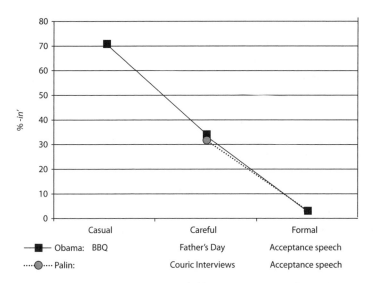

80

70

60

50

% -in' 40

30

20

10

0

Casual   Careful   Formal

—■— Obama: BBQ   Father's Day   Acceptance speech

····◯···· Palin: Couric Interviews   Acceptance speech

FIGURE 4. Sarah Palin's use of (ING) superimposed on President Obama's.

obeying the same norms for the variable (ING) as those that govern the speech of President Obama.

The Consensus

This consensus is publicly available and, in one sense, understood by all. In the classroom or on the pulpit, people will attribute the use of the *-in'* form to laziness, ignorance, or just plain rascality. Yet the high value we put on the *-in'* norm in other contexts is not hidden from public view. When we see the large illuminated sign, DUNKIN' DONUTS, we recognize the claim that *dunkin'* doughnuts taste better than *dunking* doughnuts. The *-in'* form, as we have seen, is associated with home language, and DUNKIN' DONUTS calls upon the general belief that home cooking is better than commercial cooking. Many other firms make heavy investment in the apostrophe. A Philadelphia travel agency is named with an electric sign spelling out CRUISIN'. We understand this as an advertisement that we will have a better time *cruisin'* than we would *cruising*.

To sum up, people do not speak in an unpredictable and chaotic way, in New York City or elsewhere. The *-in'* variant does not represent a loss of control, laziness, or ignorance. It alternates with *-ing* as a stable linguistic variable. People throughout the country use the -*in'* form more when they are speaking informally, less when they are speaking formally. People with more power, education, and money use -*in'* less often than people who rank lower on these dimensions of social life. We sum up these findings by saying that the variable (ING) is stratified by style and social class, evaluated by social consensus, and available for public discussion. It operates very much the same way throughout the English-speaking world.[5] As far as we know, the variation between -*in'* and -*ing* dates back to the 9th century AD.[6]

Most importantly, the (ING) variable is a prototypical example of orderly heterogeneity. It does not interfere with communication: we know that *working* and *workin'*, *dunking* and *dunkin'*, mean the same thing. Furthermore, the variation of (ING) works for us to establish levels of formality and informality and in any given context; the level of -*in'* also tells us something about the social status of the speaker. In a word, we understand (ING). That does not prevent us from attacking Sarah Palin for "dropping her g's." Public rhetoric about language behavior is always several stages removed from reality. Because we understand what (ING) is all about, we can always pick it up and use it as a club to beat our opponents on the head and shoulders with, linguistically speaking.

3 ←→ HIDDEN DIVERSITY

We are now ready to turn to a different kind of linguistic variation, which differs from (ING) on each of several counts. Instead of stability, we find rapid changes across generations; instead of universal use across the English-speaking world, changes confined to a single dialect area; instead of a topic for public debate, features that are entirely unconscious and never discussed in public. While (ING) did not interfere with communication, these changes do so, in ways that are rarely recognized. The changes in progress to be discussed in this chapter are indeed mysterious: they challenge us to search for the causes of such linguistic disruption, and to understand why people speak as they do.

As we turn to these recent changes in progress, the focus will be on the sounds of language rather than words, the forms of words, or their combinations in syntactic structure. Current changes in progress are generally limited to changes in sound patterns. Speakers of the regional dialects of North American English now differentiate themselves primarily by their vowel systems, not their grammatical systems, which turn out to be quite stable.[1] There is of course a great deal of fluctuation in vocabulary. We all find it interesting to learn that what is called *soda* in one place is called *pop* in another place, and *coke* in another. Yet the change of one word does not tell us much about change in another, and the long list of words that differ from one place to another does not form a coherent pattern or give us much insight into the machinery of speaking and listening.

The sound changes in question were first discovered in exploratory interviews in Chicago in the late 1960s and early 1970s. I was talking to a teenager named Tony about a friend of his named Marty who almost got killed. He said, "Marty, he got caught in the lax." It was only after listening to the tape several times that I figured out that Marty had got caught swimming in the *locks* leading to Lake Michigan. This was only one of a set of sound changes that we came to recognize as the "Northern Cities Shift." Later, we encountered speakers from Detroit, Buffalo, and Rochester who showed similar vowel systems.[2]

To acquaint you with these sound changes, I will draw from a series of experiments on cross-dialectal comprehension designed to see if these changes did in fact interfere with communication.[3] In Chicago, Philadelphia, and Birmingham, we recorded conversations with advanced speakers of the local dialect—young women in community colleges. We identified words that were in the forefront of change, and played them to subjects in three forms: first as isolated words, then in a phrase, and finally in the full context. When the 31 subjects from Philadelphia listened to the first item, 90% identified the word as "black." When they heard the same word in the phrase context "living on one _____," a minority of 39% changed their minds and decided it must be the word "block." When they heard it in the full context, "senior citizens living on one _____," a majority of 79% switched over to "block," but 21% still stayed with their original choice, "black." Most of the subjects came to realize that the speaker they heard was pronouncing the word "block" in the way that they themselves said "black." When the same experiment was repeated in Birmingham, Alabama, the results were more dramatic—only 3% identified the isolated word correctly.

You might think that this has no serious consequences for communication, because people from Philadelphia and Birmingham don't spend that much time in Chicago. But the pattern was not radically different for Chicago listeners. In isolated words, Chicago college students were no better than the out of towners—only 2% identified the word correctly. With more context, they did catch up and pass the others. Ninety-seven percent identified the word as *block* in the full context.

It is extraordinary that the listeners in these experiments are the same group as the speakers: first-year students in local universities.

The pronunciations that they do not recognize are their own. We must assume that college students have been exposed to the norms of other dialects, and have come to expect less-local speech forms in formal situations like this experiment. For the local listeners, a little context brought them back to the reality. Yet 20% to 30% of the out-of-town listeners still could not believe that the word intended was what the context told them it was: "block."

The experiments showed similar patterns of recognition rates for four other words. Chicago *that* was frequently heard as "theater," "Fiat," or "Peter." Only a small minority heard it as a short-a word in isolation. The word *steady* was consistently heard as "study" by most of the listeners: only 8% of the Chicagoans got the word right.

Most spectacular was the mishearing of Chicago *buses*. In isolation, the great majority of listeners heard it as "bosses." In the phrase "the *BUSES* with the antennas," there was little change; very few listeners identified the word correctly in the context: "the *BUSES* with the antennas on top." Even the Chicago listeners persisted in identifying this word as "boss" or "bosses," in spite of the fact that "boss" made no sense. Only 31% picked up the intended meaning of "buses." The majority could not believe that someone would pronounce *bus* to sound like "boss," even though this was the spontaneous production of one of their classmates.

Finally, we note that the word *talks* can be heard in isolation as "toxic," though in the full context, "We had all these conversations and *TALKS* about it," most listeners got it right.

It's important to establish now that these various changes are not disconnected events. There is a connectedness to it all that will help us understand what is happening. The five sound changes form a complete, circular chain known as the "Northern Cities Shift," as shown in figure 5. Each of the word classes—*bat, got, bought, bet,* and *but*—shift one unit along the chain.

Figure 5 displays the five vowels in a two-dimensional space. The vertical dimension is labeled "high-low," indicating whether the tongue is high or low in the mouth when the vowel is formed. The horizontal dimension is labeled "front-back," indicating whether the high point of the tongue is toward the front or the back of the mouth.

The logic that connects these five changes resembles a game of

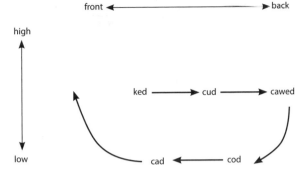

FIGURE 5. The Northern Cities Shift.

"musical chairs," in which each inhabitant of a position moves one unit to dislodge the next. The initiating event appears to be the shift of short-a in *bat* to a front, raised position, a sound very much like the vowel of *yeah*. It is not just this one word *bat* involved, but all words spelled with short-a: *cad, bad, that, cat, attitude, cap, happen, happening,* etc. This raising of short-a is familiar to speakers of any North American dialect when it is followed by a nasal consonant *m* or *n*. In the most extreme form, the girl's name *Ann* is pronounced like the boy's name *Ian*. But in Chicago, all short-a words undergo this change; there are no words in this class that retain the original sound of short-a that is heard in the *cat, bat, sat* of many other dialects.

Into the gap created by this shift, the vowel of *got* moves forward. In the most extreme form, *cot* sounds like *cat, block* like *black, socks* like *sacks*. This shift of short-o creates a new vacancy in the phonetic space that it used to occupy: there is no longer a short vowel in the low back slot. The vowel of *bought* then moves down and front toward this position, along with other members of the "long open-o" word class: *law, talk, cross, dawn, dog,* etc.[4] On the other hand, the fronted and raised short-a class has moved dangerously close to short-e. Short-e then shifts to the back toward short-u, producing a confusion between *desk* and *dusk* as short-e enters the short-u territory. Most recently, short-u has responded to this intrusion by moving back, producing the potential confusion between *buses* and *bosses, cud* and *cawed*. As noted above, the class of *bosses, talk,* and *cawed* has shifted down and front. The chain shift has come full circle.

The confusion that we observe in experimental settings is not the only sign of interference with communication produced by the Northern Cities Shift. The research team engaged in the study of cross-dialectal comprehension collected some 900 examples of misunderstandings in everyday settings. We provided our collaborators with printed forms for recording such misunderstandings immediately after they happened, and for noting crucial information that would help us determine what led to the breakdown in communication. Especially important was how long it took for the misunderstanding to be detected. In some reports, it was before the other person had finished speaking. In many cases the misunderstanding was uncovered by an immediate request for clarification. But in other cases it might not be discovered until many days later, as the result of new information that led the person to realize that a misunderstanding had taken place. The standard printed form looked like this:

MISUNDERSTANDINGS   Date _____

Speaker _____   Hearer _____

Dialect area _____   _____

Speaker said [continue on back for full setting]:

Hearer heard:

Hearer corrected mishearing after _____ sec _____ min

_____ before utterance was over

_____ by speaker's response to look or query

_____ by inference from further utterances

_____ by accidental events that followed

It turned out that misunderstandings parallel to our experimental confusions of *block* with *black* are quite common in everyday life. A linguist from the East Coast was driving through Chicago when she heard on the radio, "The Edens Expressway is jammed salad." It took her quite a few minutes to realize what had in fact been said. Another linguist, raised in Cincinnati, was listening to a radio broadcast from Oshkosh; she heard a factory worker say, "The plant doesn't get enough orders to maintain aberrations." It was not until some time later in the broadcast that she stopped wondering why the plant would want to maintain aberrations, and understood that he had said *operations*. A Canadian phonetician heard a student from St. Louis say, "I did the casting for a play," but only after he asked her how she got that job did he come to understand that she had done the *costumes* for that play.

A woman from Kansas recorded a misunderstanding between her Kansas-raised sister and a Michigan-raised cousin, in a discussion of what kinds of things can go into a dishwasher. She could not understand why the Michigander was ready to put *chapsticks* into the machine, until she finally realized that it was *chopsticks* that he had in mind. This confusion of short-o with short-a can become encapsulated in print. A Michigan newspaper reported a local politician as saying he was sure whose "ax would be gored." It is of course possible that a series of misunderstandings has led to the use of *ax* in this fixed expression, but somewhere along the line we must infer the misunderstanding of *ox* as *ax*. A linguist from the East Coast, staying at a Chicago hotel, was informed that coffee would be served every morning next to the "padded plant," and it took some time for her to realize what that was and where to look for her coffee.

The misunderstanding can operate in the opposite direction, where speakers of the Northern Cities Shift interpret the short-a of outsiders as intending short-o. The same linguist asked an employee of a Lansing branch of the Target stores where she could find "baby sleep sacks"; the clerk pointed to a display of white socks. Several days later, this misunderstanding was replayed in a branch of J. C. Penney.[5] An easterner wrote to me, "Neither my boyfriend Dave nor I are natives to Michigan. Dave had the following misunderstanding happen three times in the Lansing area, at two different grocery stores, with two different workers: he asked for 'catfish' and the man behind the counter gave him cod, thinking he said *codfish*."

The schema of the Northern Cities Shift in figure 5 indicates that short-e words can be misheard as short-u as the result of the backing of the *e* class. A traveler from Long Island heard a woman from Milwaukee say, "They couldn't find the best," and asked her, "What do you mean, the bus?" A phonetician who went to work for Motorola in Chicago was on the commuter train one morning and overheard a commuter say, "I've got a mutual fund coming in." This didn't sound so strange to him, given that many of the people on the train were financial folks. He then heard the speaker clarify to her associate, who had also misperceived the utterance: she had a mutual *friend* coming in.

The same Canadian phonetician mentioned above was walking alongside a woman from Madison, Wisconsin, who was pushing her bike and talking about where she got it from. He heard her say, "They make trucks in Wisconsin," which seemed quite irrelevant, but it was only a matter of seconds before he realized that she meant the bicycle brand Treks.

In the course of collecting this large body of misunderstandings we found that more than a quarter—27%—were the result of sound changes in one dialect or another. Since most of our observers were located in the East, the number of misunderstandings triggered by the Northern Cities Shift was relatively small. But it was enough to confirm the results of our experiments: that sound change led to a significant reduction in the capacity of language to do its main job of communicating meaning.

Who Speaks This Way?

The Northern Cities Shift was first identified in exploratory interviews in Chicago, Detroit, and Buffalo. From these and the more extensive studies of New York City and Philadelphia, there emerged a profile of the most extreme speakers of these regional dialects. They are upwardly mobile young women, in the second and third generation of newly arrived ethnic groups, with dense connections within the local neighborhood, and multiple social relations outside the neighborhood as well. In addition, one can say that the leaders of linguistic change are nonconformists, who are not afraid to defy social conventions, and social activists, ready to intervene when they see something going wrong and quick to respond to perceived injustice.[6]

Here is a narrative from an interview in Chicago in 1971 by Benji Wald with a 23-year-old, Carol M., who shows a very advanced form of the Northern Cities Shift for that time. The words that show these advanced sound changes are highlighted in italics.

BW: You used to get in some fights, huh? Tell me about one time you got in a fight.

CM: My girl friend *Deb* told me she was sittin' up in the living room, her and Gary. And this *Red* O'Malley kid liked Gary at the time. She's—I'd say she was jealous, that's what I'd say she was. And she *says*, "Go on Gary, she's a whore. You can do whatever you want to her."

So Deb told me all about it the next day, and I talked to Gary. And Monday, we went up to 103rd and *Pulaski*, because there's this pizza parlor up there and they always hung around there. So Gary went and called *Red* over, and they started arguing in the car.

So *Deb's* sittin' there *yellin'* at *Red*, sayin' "What you call me?" an' all this. An' Gary's yellin' at *Red*. An' I'm jus' keepin' quiet, you know. I just sat in the car. So Deb says, "Are we gonna fight or not? So come on."

"O.K."

So Red had on a pair of *slacks* an' everything, and *Deb* had on a *dress*. So I didn't like the idea of her getting' dirt all over it. So I opened up the window, and I said, "Do you wanna fight me? Since she's got a *dress* on?" And she says "OK." So I take off my *jacket*. I had on a turtle *neck*, it was a knit shirt, you know, and everything of my brothers. An' she sort of shied away, because she saw how big I was an' everything.

An', she swung at me first. And she hit me in the eye, and my eye got kinda *swelled* up pretty good because I just through a fight two weeks ago and I had a *black* eye out o' that one. So I jus' started swingin' an' everything, and there were these bicycles an' I threw her down over them. An' she sorta got hurt. An' I don' know why I kicked her, but I kicked her in the mouth, and she sorta got a bloody nose and it got all over her suit. An' it was a really cute suit, and I really liked it, but it was all full of blood. An' I got up. And I got her up by the *hand*. And I started *smackin'* her I. I don' know why I do these things, but everybody told me about it afterwards. 'Cause I thought I kicked her in the stomach, to tell you the truth, but I *guess* my foot went up a little bit more.

An' I *grabbed* her by the hair, and I said, "If I ever hear you callin' any of my girl *friends* a whore, you're gonna really find your *ass* all over the ground. An' she says, "Oh. . . you!" And so I started *smackin'* her *again*. I *said*, "You can get anybody you want to, but you say anything about me or anybody else that I like, whoever, you're gonna be pickin' yourself off the ground, pretty much, you know." So *that* sorta' *ended that.*

Another sample of the style of the leading exponents of linguistic change can be drawn from an interview with Jackie G. in Chicago by Sherry Ash in 1971, in connection with the project on cross-dialectal comprehension.

SA: How old are you?

JG: Ah . . . 19. I have a fake ID . . . that, uh, a police officer by the way gave me, we won't mention his name.

SA: Give me the story about it.

JG: Well my *girlfriend* goes to Illinois State University out in Normal, Illinois, and *met* a policeman out there who gave us—he confiscated these IDs from other girls, and says, "Take this *back* to *Chicago* and put it to use." And it *happens* that this girl looks like me, she's *got* the brown eyes, the brown hair, the height, the weight, so all's I did was memorize the social security number and their *address*, and it's fine, it gets me *everywhere*. I mean I don't take it—I don't go out crazy, in this bar, like I *walk* out staggering, I—you know. I know I have my limits. . . .

Where Is the Northern Cities Shift to Be Found?

The experiments on cross-dialectal comprehension focused on Chicago, where the two speakers just cited were located. As we collected data on natural misunderstandings it became evident that the Northern Cities Shift was active in a much broader region. How widespread is the Northern Cities Shift and what are its limits?

To answer this question, we turn first to the analysis of American dialects as first developed by Hans Kurath in the Atlantic seaboard states. In his first study of regional vocabulary, published in 1949, Kurath found that the usual division of the American dialects into North and South was not adequate: the data pointed to a three-way division into North, Midland, and South (fig. 6). The North is the area of original Yankee settlement from southeastern England (D. H. Fischer 1989), marked by such vocabulary items as *spider* for "frying pan," *teeter-totter* for "see-saw," *darning needle* for "dragon fly." The Midland is an area of largely Scots-Irish settlement, centering on Philadelphia in the East, and expanding to cover much of the Midwest. The Midland vocabulary opposes *bucket* to Northern *pail* and *mosquito hawk* to *darning needle* for "dragon fly."

Kurath and McDavid's mapping of the pronunciation of English in the Atlantic states (1961) found North/Midland/South divisions along the same boundary lines. Most speakers in the North and in the South distinguished *which* from *witch;* the Midland speakers did not. Most of the North and the South distinguished *four* from *for, hoarse* from *horse, mourning* from *morning;* the Midland did not.

Until recently, the only systematic mapping of North American pronunciation was confined to the Atlantic states. The North/Midland/South distinction was extended westward to the Great Plains area on the basis of studies of regional vocabulary (Shuy 1962; Carver 1987), but no overall view of the dialect geography of American sound patterns was available. We noted above that the Northern Cities Shift was first discovered in 1972 in exploratory studies of Rochester, Buffalo, Detroit, and Chicago.[7] Though this pointed to a northern origin, it was not possible to say how general the shift was, or how it corresponded to Kurath's divisions, until the publication of the *Atlas of North American English* by Labov, Ash, and Boberg in 2006. This work provided the first overall view of the pronunciation of English on the North American continent, based on a telephone survey of 762 speakers in the mid-1990s. It maps the vowel systems of all 223 North American cities with a population of over 50,000.

Figure 7 shows the dialects of North American English as defined by the *Atlas*. While figure 6 is based on regional vocabulary, the boundaries of figure 7 are formed by the outer limits of the active sound changes in progress. The areas marked North, Midland, and South coincide generally with the westward extension of the vocabulary of the three main regions of figure 6. As we will see, this is the result of the steady westward orientation of streams of settlement in the 19th century. Within the North on figure 7 is a smaller area labeled Inland North. Below this is the Midland, now separated from the eastern seaboard by the distinctively different dialects of Pittsburgh and Philadelphia.[8] In the Kurath map in figure 6, Appalachia is included in the Midland, but in figure 7 it forms part of the South. Within the South, two areas of maximal advancement of Southern sound changes are labeled Inland South and Texas South.

We can now answer the question, where is the Northern Cities Shift to be found? It is the speech pattern of the Inland North. Though

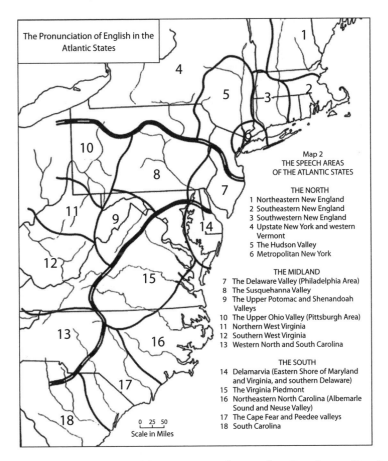

The Pronunciation of English in the Atlantic States

4

5 3 2

1

10

8

7

11 9 14

12

15

13 16

17

18

Map 2
THE SPEECH AREAS
OF THE ATLANTIC STATES

THE NORTH
1 Northeastern New England
2 Southeastern New England
3 Southwestern New England
4 Upstate New York and western Vermont
5 The Hudson Valley
6 Metropolitan New York

THE MIDLAND
7 The Delaware Valley (Philadelphia Area)
8 The Susquehanna Valley
9 The Upper Potomac and Shenandoah Valleys
10 The Upper Ohio Valley (Pittsburgh Area)
11 Northern West Virginia
12 Southern West Virginia
13 Western North and South Carolina

THE SOUTH
14 Delamarvia (Eastern Shore of Maryland and Virginia, and southern Delaware)
15 The Virginia Piedmont
16 Northeastern North Carolina (Albemarle Sound and Neuse Valley)
17 The Cape Fear and Peedee valleys
18 South Carolina

0 25 50
Scale in Miles

FIGURE 6. Dialect areas of the eastern United States (from Kurath 1949; Kurath and McDavid 1961).

this territory is smaller than the North as a whole, it is actually a vast area bordering the Great Lakes, extending eastward to cover most of New York State, and westward into northern Illinois, southern Wisconsin, and eastern Iowa. The Inland North is a subset of the larger Northern area, which extends the vocabulary and sound patterns of the North in figure 6, and is marked by the phonetic conditions that make the Northern Cities Shift possible.[9] The line between the Inland North and the Midland runs below the Western Reserve in Ohio, south of Toledo, veers northward to near the upper border of Indiana, and then passes below the northern third of Illinois and above the

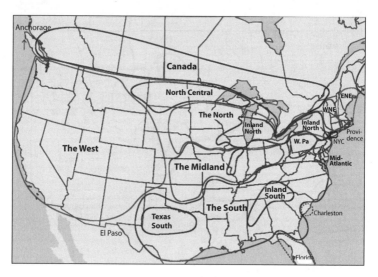

FIGURE 7. Dialects of North American English as defined in the *Atlas* (from map 11.15).

lower third of Iowa. Though it is not prominent in public conscious-ness, the North/Midland boundary is the deepest division in the phonology of the United States. Dozens of words in the traditional rural vocabulary differentiate the North from the Midland along this boundary. Northern *pail* corresponds to Midland *bucket;* Northern *spider* to Midland *skillet;* Northern *sawbuck* to Midland *trestle.* Many of these regional terms have become obsolete. But in our studies of the sound systems of the North and the Midland, we find 10 different features that bundle together, differentiating the North from the Mid-land in a uniform way.[10]

The Northern Cities Shift is found in all the cities of western New York State: Utica, Syracuse, Rochester, and Buffalo; in Cleveland, Ellyria, Massillon, and Toledo in Ohio; in Detroit, Ann Arbor, Flint, Grand Rapids, and Kalamazoo in Michigan; in Chicago, Rockford, and Joliet in Illinois; in Madison, Kenosha, and Milwaukee in southeast-ern Wisconsin. The Northern Cities Shift is identified not only with these but with every city in this region (Gordon 2000, 2001; Plichta and Rakerd 2002; Thomas 2010). Inland North is the urban concen-tration of Northern speakers, a vast conurbation of 88,000 square miles, with a population of over 34 million.

On the other hand, cities of the Midland—Columbus, Indianapolis, Kansas City, Omaha—show no signs of the Northern Cities Shift.

Acoustic Measurements

In order to follow the progress of the Northern Cities Shift, we make use of acoustic analysis. The *Atlas* was based on 134,000 such measurements, which track vowel quality through the central tendencies of bands of high energy in the spectrum of the vowel called *formants*. The location of the first formant is closely correlated with the height of the vowel in terms of tongue position, and the second formant gives us an indication of the position of the vowel on the front-back dimension. These measurements are considerably more precise and reliable than estimates of tongue position made by ear, that is, by impressionistic phonetics.[11] Thus the raising of short-a corresponds to lower values of the first formant and the backing of short-u corresponds to lower values of the second formant.

Using such measures, we trace the geographic outlines and internal consistency of the Northern Cities Shift (NCS) to see how it evolved. The examples I have used so far are drawn from the most advanced users of these sound changes. At this point, we need a more general criterion, one that separates all those engaged in the Northern Cities Shift from others. Since the NCS involves a complex movement of five vowels, measures of its progress call for calculations of positions relative to each other, rather than the position of individual vowels. As we have seen, the NCS involves the fronting of short-o in *got, socks,* and *block* to sound like *gat, sacks,* and *black* and the backing of short-u in *but, bus,* and *bunk* to sound like *bought, boss,* and *bonk.* For most dialects, short-u is a central vowel and short-o is a back vowel, but under the influence of the NCS, they reverse their relative positions on the front-back dimension. Figure 8 maps this aspect of the NCS by what we will call the *UD criterion:* whether short-u in *but* is pronounced farther back in the mouth than short-o in *got* or the reverse. The solid circles indicate speakers for whom the UD criterion holds: mean measures of the second formant (F2) show that short-u is pronounced farther back in the mouth than short-o. The empty circles indicate all those speakers for whom short-u is farther front than short-o.

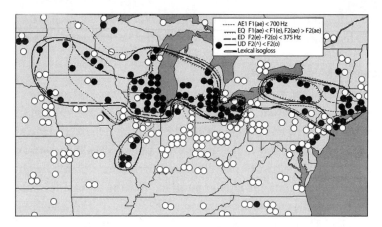

F IGURE 8. The homogeneity of the Northern Cities Shift in the Inland North as indicated by the UD criterion: *cud* is further back than *cawed* (from *Atlas*, map 14.11). See note 12 for explanation of legend.

Figure 8 clearly defines the southern boundary of the Inland North. The outer boundaries of three other measures of the NCS are shown as well.[12] The Inland North is then that inner area where all of these measures coincide. Within that inner area, the UD measure shows an extraordinary homogeneity: figure 8 shows only 3 white circles inside the Inland North boundary out of 58. Below the North/Midland line we see only white circles, except for the narrow corridor leading down to St. Louis[13] and a scattering of four points in the extreme eastern territory of the mid-Atlantic region.

The North Diverging from the Midland

The fact that almost everyone in the North has adopted this back pronunciation in *but* and *bunk* does not in itself point to divergence, the major theme of this book. It might be that short-u has been relatively back since the earliest period of settlement of the North and relatively front from the earliest settlement of the area to the south, the Midland. We can check this by taking advantage of the wide range of ages among the *Atlas* subjects to see if there is change in "apparent time"— that is, are younger speakers pronouncing these words farther back than older speakers in the same region? Figure 9 accordingly plots the backness of short-u words against age for each speaker in the Inland North and the Midland. The vertical axis is the mean value of the second formant (F2) for short-u. At the top of the scale the value is 1800; this produces a sound closer to short-e than short-u, so that *bunk* is close to *benk* and *bunch* to *bench*. At the bottom of the scale, where F2 is as low as 1200, *bunk* sounds like *bonk*. The horizontal axis shows age of the *Atlas* subjects, from 12 to 78. Inland North speakers are shown as open circles and Midland speakers as dark squares. The two lines are partial trend lines for age for each dialect area: the solid line for the North, the dashed line for the Midland. For the older speakers on the right, it is evident that there is no difference between the North and the Midland. But the values for North and Midland become steadily more different as we examine younger speakers, until there is no overlap at all for speakers age 20 and below.

There are two possible explanations for such an age pattern. It may be that this is a stable situation, and that in every generation, young people in the Midland use fronter forms of short-u and young people in the North use backer forms, and that as they grow older, both groups shift toward a common mean value. But this is not likely. We have real-time data, recordings made in the 1960s in Chicago, which show no such backing of short-u among young people. The

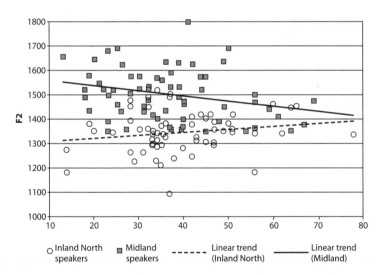

FIGURE 9. Divergence in the fronting and backing of short-u by age for the Inland North and the Midland.

most likely interpretation of figure 9 is that this view of change in apparent time is a reflection of change in real time, and that the two regions are drifting further apart in their pronunciation of short-u as time goes on.

This view of change in real time is strongly reinforced by the results of a recent study of the durability of the North/Midland boundary in Ohio by Erik Thomas (2010). Thomas analyzed the older speakers recorded for the *Dictionary of American Regional English* in 1965–70, with birth dates from 1880 to 1907. He compared these with 42 younger speakers that he interviewed himself in 2006–8, with birth dates from 1970 through 1994. The vowels that he studied included three of the five involved in the Northern Cities Shift. Thomas concludes:

> The results of this study show that the old Northern-Midland boundary
> established by settlement patterns of the early nineteenth century has
> been preserved to a great extent in vowel variation. In fact, vowel
> variants seem to mark the boundary more distinctly than they did in
> the past. (419)

Why Is This Happening?

This display of language change in progress poses two questions for explanation. What can account for the uniform direction of change throughout the vast area of the Inland North? Secondly, what accounts for the sharpness of the boundary between the North and the Midland? One possibility is that this reflects discontinuities in communication networks: that the people in the Inland North form one linguistic community and the people in the Midland another, and as a result of this discontinuity they are simply drifting apart.

The most prominent linguist of the 1930s, Leonard Bloomfield, developed this explanation for the location of dialect boundaries:

> Every speaker is constantly adapting his speech-habits to those of his in-
> terlocutors. . . . When any innovation in the way of speaking spreads over
> a district, the limit of this spread is sure to be along some lines of weak-
> ness in the network of oral communication, and these lines of weakness,
> in so far as they are topographical lines, are the boundaries between
> towns, villages, and settlements. (1933, 476)

Bloomfield's speculation was based on a thought experiment that recorded every act of communication between all members of the community. Though he did not think that such a study could really be accomplished, it can be done today by the use of various indicators of communication. In an earlier study, I used state reports of average daily traffic flow on their main highways to trace the flow of communication across the eastern United States (Labov 1974). I found that most of the boundaries identified by traditional dialect geography did indeed correspond to low points in the network of communication. More recently, Dirk Brockmann and colleagues at Northwestern University have tracked communication patterns through the movements of currency, as shown by nine million reports on the online bill-tracking page, wheresgeorge.com. The network of dollar-bill flux shows the amount of communication between each 2 of the 3,109 counties of the United States by these records of exchange of dollar bills.[14] In the major patterns of communication that emerge, the various cities of the Inland North are linked to different networks. The cities of New York State—Utica, Rochester, Syracuse, and Buffalo—are directly connected to New York City. But most other cities of the Inland North—Cleveland, Detroit, Flint, Milwaukee—are linked to Chicago. Furthermore, the Chicago network reaches across the North/Midland line to the Midland cities of Columbus, Dayton, and Indianapolis. We find no reflection here of linguistic boundaries in the communication patterns. In fact, most of the traffic flow is across the North/Midland boundary. It follows that the differences in pronunciation between the North and the Midland are not due to a lack of communication across that boundary. So we must look for some other explanation of this growing separation of the North and Midland dialects.

In chapter 2 we saw that sociolinguistic variables can be stable over time and across generations and regions, establishing a common stratification by style and social class. In contrast, the recent linguistic changes that increase diversity are stratified by age and regionally differentiated, with little differentiation across styles or social classes. These new linguistic changes lie far below the level of social awareness and are never mentioned in public discussions. Most importantly, they challenge our understanding of why people behave as they do. What then are the causes of this increasing linguistic diversity?

One way of looking at it is purely mechanical. The chain shifts of vowels can be compared to trains moving in opposite directions. Most of the vowels shifts that we are considering here are unidirectional; they are not likely to back up and reverse. In my recently completed volume 3 of *Principles of Linguistic Change* (Labov 2010a), over half of the chapters are devoted to a structural accounting of how one change engages another. But such structural descriptions do not yield an understanding of the driving forces that keep the changes moving to achieve the radical dislocation that we see here. This is perhaps the most long-standing and puzzling question of linguistics. In 1856 the Indo-European scholar Rudolph von Raumer summed up the state of current knowledge in this way:

> We ascertain that the sounds of words have changed when we compare the older state of languages with the more recent. The process of the change itself however has not yet been investigated enough. If we penetrate deeper into the darkness which in many ways veils these questions, we find a huge multitude of highly different processes at work. (1967, 67–86)

Some 50 years later, Saussure reviewed the situation in similar terms:

> The search for the causes of phonetic changes is one of the most difficult problems of linguistics. Many explanations have been proposed, but none of them thoroughly illuminates the problem. (1959, 147)

Finally, we may quote Bloomfield, writing in 1933:

> Although many sound-changes shorten linguistic forms, simplify the phonetic system, or in some other way lessen the labor of utterance, yet no student has succeeded in establishing a correlation between sound-change and any antecedent phenomenon: the causes of sound-change are unknown.

Is There Convergence as Well as Divergence?

The recent development of diversity in the Inland North, headed by the Northern Cities Shift, is not unique. The *Atlas of North American English* shows vigorous new sound changes in Canada, the mid-

Atlantic states, western Pennsylvania, the Midland, and the West. The dialects of Chicago, Philadelphia, Pittsburgh, and Los Angeles are now more different from each other than they were 50 or 100 years ago. The metropolitan dialects of Boston and New York appear to be stable. On the other hand, dialects of many smaller cities have receded in favor of the new regional patterns. The unique dialect of Charleston has given way to a general Midland form (Baranowski 2007), and so has the dialect of Cincinnati (Boberg and Strassel 2000). St. Louis is abandoning its traditional merger of *far* and *for, card* and *cord,* and has adopted many features of the Northern Cities Shift (Labov 2007). We find that the dialect of the South is on the whole slowly receding: younger speakers everywhere in the South are shifting away from the marked features of Southern speech (*Atlas,* chap. 18). The study of remnant dialects in isolated coastal communities shows movements in both directions (Wolfram and Schilling-Estes 2004). In Ocracoke, on the Outer Banks of North Carolina, the traditional pronunciation that has led the residents to be called Hoi Toiders is receding among younger speakers. In Smith Island, in Chesapeake Bay, it is intensifying.

One of the most striking examples of convergence is the importation of consonantal /r/ into the "r-less" dialects of the eastern United States. In the traditional pattern of these dialects, /r/ after a vowel is pronounced as an extension of the vowel, often followed by a glide, as in the well-known oratorical style of Franklin Roosevelt. In this system, words spelled as *car* are pronounced as "cah" unless the next word begins with a vowel. This was not the type of speech imported from England when the colonies were first settled. The first evidence we have for this r-less British speech is found in Walker's Dictionary of 1795, representing the London pronunciation that is still dominant both in the standard Received Pronunciation and in Cockney. In the first part of the 19th century, this r-less pattern was adopted by almost all the eastern seaboard cities of the United States: Boston, Providence, New York, Richmond, Charleston, and Savannah. On the East Coast, only Philadelphia resisted this trend, reflecting its Scots-Irish settlement history and its position as the center of resistance to British influence.

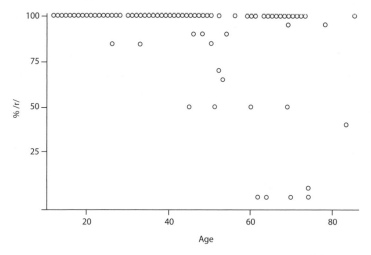

FIGURE 10. Rapid advancement of r-ful pronunciation in the South by age among white *Atlas* subjects in the 1990s.

Shortly after the end of World War II, this norm was reversed. Speakers in the r-less cities began to pronounce final /r/ in careful speech, just as they pronounce final -*ing* (Labov 1966). The effect on everyday speech has been more extreme in the South, where the records of the *Atlas* show an overwhelming shift to r-pronunciation among young people. Figure 10 shows this Southern pattern for white subjects. The horizontal axis is age and the vertical axis the percentage of pronunciation of /r/ as a consonant. There is no r-lessness among people under 40 in formerly r-less Richmond, Columbia, or Mobile: all the speakers in that age range are at the 100% level.

The Overall View of Divergence and Convergence

The general picture of North American dialects shows both convergence and divergence, as local dialects give way to regional dialects. But except for the South, those regional dialects show no signs of giving way to the influence of the mass media, and they all display new and vigorous sound changes in progress. Chapters 6 and 7 will plunge further into the question of what is driving these new developments, and search for some answers that will fit the vast scope and uniformity of the sound changes described here.

Before we begin the inquiry into this question, we must confront the fact that the view of American English dialects presented so far is incomplete. It is drawn from a mapping of the mainstream white dialects. We have to acknowledge another, deeper division in the language, between these mainstream white dialects and the speech of African Americans, who participate only marginally in these sound changes but join instead in the development of a dialect that moves off in an entirely different direction—African American Vernacular English. The next chapter will follow that direction and ask why this should be so.

4 ↔ THE GROWING DIVERGENCE OF BLACK AND WHITE ENGLISH

Chapter 3 looked at the increasing divergence of the regional dialects of English, and posed the questions of why and how this unexpected situation came about. Before pursuing this issue, I have to face the fact that so far the diversity of American dialects has been grossly understated. The racial divide between black and white forms of English is much deeper than the regional differentiation across the North/Midland boundary.

African American Vernacular English

When we study the language of any large American city, we find that a majority of the African American population speak a dialect very different from the rest of the population. This form of English has been variously called "Black English," "Ebonics," and "African American English." Linguists generally call it African American Vernacular English or AAVE. Any public discussion of this form of English generates emotional waves whose violence cannot be overestimated. The next chapter, on the politics of AAVE, will portray in some detail the history of those public firestorms. This chapter begins with the linguistic view of the matter: that AAVE is a dialect of English which, like all other vernaculars, is governed by a complex set of systematic rules, with all of the structures needed for logical expression and learning.

One question to be asked in this exploration of dialect diversity in America is whether African Americans participate in the regional differences that were displayed in the last chapter. To answer this question, I will draw upon a very broad range of linguistic research. Indeed, it is often said that AAVE is the most closely studied nonstandard dialect in the world. As the name "African American *Vernacular* English" indicates, these studies are aimed at capturing the form of language that is used in everyday life among family members and close friends. They report remarkably similar sets of grammatical rules, both variable and constant, used by African Americans who for the most part talk with, live with, and work with other African Americans.

Our view of AAVE comes from sociolinguistic interviews where the topic of conversation is not language but many other matters that engage the attention and emotional concerns of the speaker. The earliest such work was done in Harlem in 1966 (Labov et al. 1968), in Detroit by Wolfram (1969), and in Washington by Fasold (1972). I led a second research group in Philadelphia in the 1980s (Labov and Harris 1986; Ash and Myhill 1986). On the West Coast, Mitchell-Kernan reported on the Bay Area (1969); a group at the Southwestern Regional Laboratory studied adolescent youth in Los Angeles (Legum et al. 1972). Baugh studied the Pacoima neighborhood in Los Angeles (1983); and Rickford directed a research group in East Palo Alto (Rickford et al. 1991). Beginning in 1991, Bailey and Cukor-Avila have carried out a yearly study of a small Texas town they called "Springville" (Bailey 1993; Cukor-Avila 1995). Anne Charity Hudley worked with schoolchildren in Washington, DC, Cleveland, and New Orleans in 2005 (Charity 2007) and has continued her work in Richmond. To these can be added the results of our recent work in reading research, which includes recordings of the spontaneous speech of over 500 elementary schoolchildren in Philadelphia, Atlanta, and California (Labov 2010b; Labov and Baker 2010).

How Uniform Is AAVE?

While chapter 3 showed that mainstream white dialects are becoming increasingly different across regions, this chapter begins with the opposite observation. AAVE shows remarkably little variation across the great cities where it is spoken. Because this is a controversial matter, it will be helpful to rely upon the recent unanimous statement by nine linguists who had done most of this research. The statement was in response to a requirement of the California Curriculum Commission, adopted April 7, 2006, for publishers to provide "additional

support for students who use African American Vernacular English."
The nine linguists (H. Samy Alim, Guy Bailey, John Baugh, Anne
Charity, Lisa Green, William Labov, John Rickford, Tracy Weldon,
Walt Wolfram) submitted their *Summary Statement on AAVE* to the
commission on February 8, 2008. This document, given as a whole
in the appendix, states,

> There are still many areas of disagreement on the origin and past his-
> tory of AAVE and there are many open questions concerning the current
> direction of its development. However, there is general agreement on
> the main sound patterns and grammatical features that distinguish this
> variety from other dialects of English. These features have often been
> found to be similar across the United States in areas with a high degree
> of residential segregation.

There are other ways to look at the situation. Some linguists use
the term "African American English" (or AAE) to designate the full
range of English used by African Americans throughout the United
States, in small towns and big cities, in the South as well as the North.
This approach emphasizes the wide range of variation to be found
among African American speakers, including a standard African
American English marked only by some features of pronunciation,
and the speech of African Americans in small rural communities,
which shows strong local influence. Wolfram (2007) prefers to view
this larger picture as a way of capturing the dynamics of the African
American English–speaking community as a whole. Furthermore, he
argues that "regionality has played a significant role in the earlier development of varieties of AAE, and it continues to play a significant
role in its development" (2007, 5).

Regional Differences in AAVE Pronunciation

Any estimate of the uniformity of AAVE must immediately be modified to say that it applies more to grammar than to pronunciation.
And since the evidence on dialect divergence presented in the last
chapter dealt entirely with the pronunciation of English rather than
its grammar, we will want to examine the relation between pronunciation variables for African Americans and the surrounding community.

Anyone familiar with the African American community will be conscious of many differences in pronunciation of AAVE from one city to the next. African Americans in East St. Louis are well known for their pronunciation of *there, where,* etc., with the vowel of *her,* a dialect feature that was highlighted in Chingy's 2003 rap single "Right thurr."

Chapter 22 of the *Atlas of North American English* is devoted to regional differences in the pronunciation of African Americans. Since the *Atlas* subjects were chosen from the dominant ethnic groups in a given city, it followed naturally enough that a majority of the 44 African American subjects were located in the South. In each southern city, African Americans differ from whites significantly. The speech of southern African Americans is best described as conservative in regard to the vowel shifts that mark the dialect of that region. They tend to preserve traditional features that are disappearing, like the distinction between *which* and *witch,* but are also more advanced in the use of new mergers, like the coincidence of *feel* and *fill.* In the North, the speech of most African Americans is marked by the merger of *pin* and *pen, him* and *hem,* a reflection of their southern heritage.

R-pronunciation among African Americans

For a more precise view of the relations of black and white pronunciation, let us consider the variable of "r-lessness" discussed at the end of the last chapter (fig. 10). This feature underlines the tendency of African Americans to preserve traditional features of regional pronunciation. The percentage of /r/ pronounced in the African American community varies from one city to another, but in all cities African Americans are more r-less than whites. Furthermore, /r/ is often dropped between two vowels, as in *Flo'ida, Ca'olina, inte'ested.* Figure 11 adds the southern African American subjects interviewed for the *Atlas* to the data on r-pronunciation of southern white speakers in figure 10. African Americans are considerably lower in r-pronunciation than others, so that the r-less area among young people is now occupied. Yet African Americans also respond to the general trend toward increasing r-pronunciation, at a lower level, as shown by the parallel trend lines. This result, based on cities with population over 50,000, makes it plain that African Americans are participating in the trends

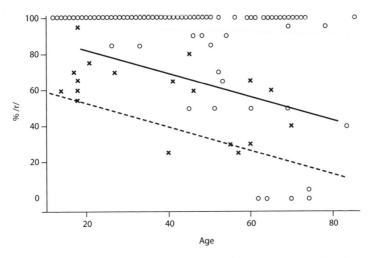

FIGURE 11. Advancement of r-ful pronunciation by age for white and black *Atlas* subjects in the South. Whites: circles, solid regression line; blacks: crosses, dashed regression line.

of the larger linguistic community, but remain distinctly differentiated from the mainstream.

We can observe a similar relation of African American r-lessness to the speech of surrounding white communities in Wolfram's study of African Americans in rural North Carolina. In figure 12, the European American community in Appalachian western North Carolina on the right shows no r-lessness, and African Americans only a small percentage of r-absence, primarily in older speakers. On the left, the European American English (EAE) of the Outer Banks on the eastern edges of the state shows a good 10% r-less pronunciation, and the three African American dialects of that area a much larger tendency in that direction. The urban shift to /r/ may not yet have reached African Americans in these small towns.

Black and White Pronunciation in Philadelphia

Alone among the major cities of the eastern seaboard, Philadelphia features an r-pronouncing dialect. African Americans, who show close to 0% /r/ in r-less New York City, average about 50% /r/ in Philadelphia (Myhill 1988). A much sharper divide appears in the vowel

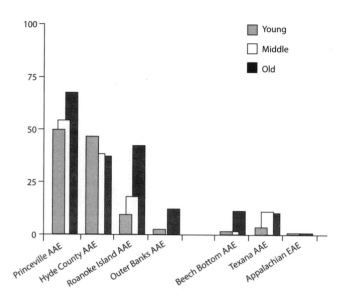

FIGURE 12. Percentage postvocalic r-lessness in regionally situated communities in North Carolina (from Wolfram 2007, fig. 2). AAE = African American English; EAE = European American English.

system of Philadelphia. One of the characteristic sounds of Philadelphia may be heard in the vowel of *south, out, about, now*. A conservative Philadelphian version of the word *out* begins with the vowel of *at* and moves toward the sound of "oat." A more advanced Philadelphian form of *out* begins with the sound of the letter "A," quickly followed by the vowel of *ought*. The word *down* is pronounced as "day" quickly followed by "awn." In Philadelphia, the word *crown* then turns out to be exactly the same as *crayon*. But African Americans in Philadelphia use none of these forms. They say *out* with a more conservative Northern diphthong that begins with the sound of "ah" and ends in "oat."

In the 1980s we conducted research in Philadelphia on the extent to which African Americans participated in the active sound changes that were characteristic of the dialect of white Philadelphians.[1] We were interested in the social significance of this difference in the pronunciation of the vowel of *out* and *about*, and carried out an experiment on how it was perceived by Philadelphians. We converted a token of the normal African American pronunciation of *get out of the house* beginning with "ah" to the conservative form used by Philadelphia whites, beginning with the vowel of "at." These two forms were embedded in a series of extracts of the speech of black and white Philadelphians. Seventy listeners—white, black, Puerto Rican—were asked to decide the ethnicity of each speaker.

Figure 13 displays the result: a dramatic reversal in ethnic identification. For all three groups of judges, the fronting of this one vowel was enough to create a strong shift in their perception of the speaker's race. It should be noted that the pronunciation of *out, south, loud,* etc., is not one of the conscious stereotypes of white speech among blacks. When blacks imitate whites, they change other vowels—and use a very long /r/—but do not pay any attention to the vowel of *out*.

In classrooms throughout Philadelphia, young black children spend five to six hours a day listening to teachers who use the white Philadelphia forms of *out* and *south*, yet they do not show any tendency to acquire this pronunciation. Only a few African American children raised in isolation from other black speakers adopt the vowel system of Philadelphia English.

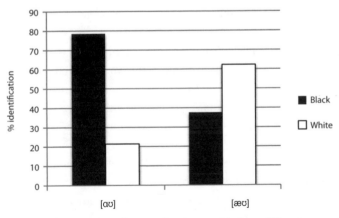

FIGURE 13. Ethnic identification of two pronunciations of "I gotta get out of the house" with original [ɑʊ] vs. acoustically fronted forms of the vowel [æʊ] in *out* and *house*.

African Americans and the Northern Cities Shift

Since the Northern Cities Shift was discovered, many studies of African American English in the North have addressed the question of whether African Americans were participating in this systematic rotation of English short vowels. A number of studies of African Americans and other minority groups in Michigan show shifts in the direction of the Northern Cities Shift but with distinct, and more limited, phonetic targets (Evans, Ito, Jones, and Preston 2006). But no further indication of the diffusion of the Northern Cities Shift appears.

The evidence so far indicates that African Americans in the Inland North do not participate in the Northern Cities Shift any more than African Americans in Philadelphia participate in Philadelphia sound changes. In the matter of pronunciation, African Americans are followers rather than leaders, and they do not follow very far. It will appear that there are many new developments in AAVE, but they are not borrowed from the surrounding white dialects. Rather, they come from deep inside the grammar of AAVE.

Where Did AAVE Come From?

Before entering into a description of AAVE grammar, it may be helpful to address the question, where did AAVE come from?

The historical origins of this dialect are a much discussed and much disputed topic (B. Bailey 1965; Stewart 1967, 1968; Dillard 1973; Fasold 1976; Baugh 1983; Bailey and Maynor 1987; Butters 1989; Bailey, Maynor, and Cukor-Avila 1991; Rickford 1980, 1999; G. Bailey 1993, 2001; Wolfram and Thomas 2002). If there is a general consensus (Labov 1982b), it is that AAVE shows strong substrate influences from the West African languages originally spoken by the slave populations. There is no doubt that the basic characteristics of the dialect are associated with the long history of African Americans in this country, and the history of slavery. Figure 14 displays the geographic history involved. Before the 18th century, the only area of the United States that had a predominant concentration of African Americans was the rice-growing plantations of the Sea Islands of the Southeast. In that area there still remains a creole language, Gullah, with strong

African influence on its grammar and vocabulary. But Gullah has only a family resemblance to AAVE, which appears to have formed at a later date. AAVE is clearly a dialect of English rather than a separate creole language. With the invention of the cotton gin by Eli Whitney in 1793, slavery became profitable over a vast agricultural area to the west and expanded through Georgia, Alabama, Mississippi, Louisiana, and Texas, with a rapid growth of the slave population. Many of the new slaves brought to this area came directly from Africa in the first third of the 19th century. A second large population movement was the Great Migration, which began just before World War I when large numbers of southern blacks took up jobs in northern cities. The African American populations of these northern cities expanded rapidly. The size of each circle in figure 14 is roughly proportional to the current African American population in the 2004 census. The end result is that the largest populations of African Americans are found not in the South but in New York, Philadelphia, Baltimore, Detroit, and Chicago, the homeland of AAVE. As we will see, this population moved into areas of each city that became increasingly segregated, with increasing poverty and unemployment. The leftmost arrows of figure 14 show a movement farther westward from Texas and Arkansas which brought African Americans to Los Angeles and the Bay Area.

It is generally agreed that there is no evidence for a full-fledged creole language in the American South as an ancestor of AAVE, aside from the distinct Gullah language in the Sea Islands. It is also clear that the speech of slaves was always different from that of their masters. Some of those differences are disappearing (Vaughn-Cooke 1986; Wolfram and Thomas 2002), and in the early decades of the study of black speech there was much discussion of an expected convergence with other dialects, or "decreolization." But most of them are extraordinarily persistent, and some of the most marked features are absolutely new.

The Structure of AAVE

The linguistic studies of AAVE cited above allow us to chart the characteristics of this dialect as it is spoken throughout the United States. This will involve variable as well as constant elements. The study

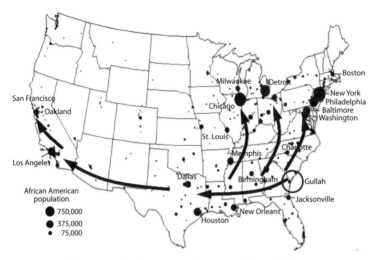

Boston
Milwaukee · Detroit
New York
San Francisco
Philadelphia
Oakland
Chicago
Baltimore
Washington

St. Louis

Los Angeles
Memphis
Charlotte

Dallas
Birmingham
Gullah

African American
population
Jacksonville

● 750,000
New Orleans
● 375,000
Houston
• 75,000

FIGURE 14. The geographic dispersion of AAVE in the United States.

of variation is the special province of sociolinguistics; we have seen some of the techniques used in tracing the variability of -ing in chapter 2. At the heart of this study lies the effort to describe the *vernacular,* a term we have already encountered in the name African American Vernacular English. The vernacular is the basic linguistic system that a child learns first, masters perfectly, and uses with unerring skill in later life with family, friends, and peers in intimate situations where minimal attention is given to speech. As speakers grow older, they acquire *superposed* dialects appropriate for more formal situations, and often these superposed dialects are defined by higher percentages of the more standard variant. This produces the pattern of figure 1, in chapter 2, where "Casual speech" on the left-hand side is the closest approximation to the vernacular that we can achieve in a recorded interview. In this case, the vernacular shows the highest percentage of the -in' variant, but variation is not eliminated. As we have seen, both the -ing and -in' form are well known to everyone (and this will include speakers of AAVE). Every speaker of English knows how and when to use each form.

All adult speakers of AAVE have the capacity to shift styles as they adjust some variable elements in their repertoire in the direction of standard English. This systematic shift is different from another kind of variation, the borrowing of elements from other dialects that do not have a consistent representation in the vernacular.

Figure 15 displays the features that represent the most important differences between AAVE and other dialects of English. On the left are elements smaller than words—grammatical suffixes that indicate the relations between words.[2] AAVE is marked by the *absence* of some of these features. On the right-hand side is a set of words that mark grammatical meanings of tense, mood, and aspect in ways that are unique to AAVE. These show the *presence* of features and meanings that are absent in other dialects. Both types of differences—absence and presence—are important in assessing the linguistic distance between AAVE and other dialects.

AAVE: Absence of Elements Found in Other Dialects

The grammatical endings listed on the left of figure 15 are of two types. In the first column are variable elements. One of these is the past tense *-ed*, as in *He walked*, which is sometimes pronounced and sometimes not in AAVE. The second is the contracted form of *is*, which is also variable, so that we sometimes hear AAVE speakers saying *He's here* and sometimes *He here*. Much linguistic research has shown that these variable elements are best understood as *deletions*—extensions of general English contraction and shortening rules, operating on elements that are present in the underlying mental

Absence of standard English suffixes		*Presence* of unique features of AAVE
Variable absence	Invariant absence	habitual *be*
		preterit *had*
Past *-ed*	Verbal *-s*	intensive perfective *done*
He walked	*He walks*	past perfective *been done*
Copula *'s*	Possessive *-s*	resultative *be done*
He's here	*John's house*	remote perfect *BIN*
(Extensions of contraction)	(Absent in the underlying grammar)	perseverative *steady*
		indignative *come*

FIGURE 15. Domains of English grammar where AAVE and standard English are most different.

grammar. The deleted elements are part of the linguistic knowledge of the speaker.[3] This is not true for the suffixes in the second column that are fundamentally absent from AAVE grammar: the verbal -s in *he walks* (AAVE *He walk*) and the possessive *'s* in *John's house* (AAVE *John house*). There is considerable evidence to show that children who grow up with AAVE as their home language do not have these elements in their grammar.

The uncertain status of verbal -s in AAVE appears most crucially in odd misplacements among sentences in which speakers of AAVE do add -s to a verb. In the Harlem study, we recorded examples (1)–(3) from adolescent speakers.

(1) He can goes out.

(2) I don't know how to gets no girls.

(3) He'd knows that.

In general English, -s can be added to the verb only when it is the first member of the verb phrase, and can register the difference between past and present. In these three examples it has been wrongly added to a verb that comes later in the verb phrase—a participle or an infinitive. We never observe such misplacements with the past tense -ed; that is, no one has reported sentences like (4) or (5).

(4) * He can tried hard.

(5) * He will passed me.

The possessive ending -s is absent in AAVE with even higher frequency than verbal -s, but here it follows a regular rule: use -s to indicate possession by a single noun or pronoun, but never between the possessor and the possessed. That is, AAVE has regular -s in *This is hers, This is mines, This is John's*, but not in *her book, my book, John book*. Thus possessive *'s* is not missing from AAVE grammar in "absolute" final position, as in *This is John's*, but it is normally absent between two nouns, as in *This is John house*.

To show how consistent this pattern can be, examples (6)–(10) show all relevant examples of two nouns related by possession from an interview with Bryan A., seven years old, a struggling reader in a West Philadelphia elementary school:

(6) If I don't get out my mom room, I get in trouble and when I don't get out my sister room she hit me.

(7) Bernicia penpal gave me one.

(8) That's what he did to my cousin Raymond dog at my cousin house.

(9) I was acting like I stole my sister food.

(10) At the museum, it was fun, we went in somebody heart.

Figure 16 displays the overall use of -s endings by Philadelphia elementary school children in our reading intervention program (Labov and Baker 2010). The African American children show 65% absence of verbal -s as in *He walks,* 60% absence of the possessive -s as in *John house,* but only 17% absence of the variable *'s* that represents an underlying *is* in *He's tired.* These interviews are lively, but they still take place in the school context, where the influence of standard English is always present; yet the grammatical pattern of the vernacular emerges strongly. By contrast, white struggling readers of the same age with the same reading problems show very little absence of the grammatical machinery of standard English.

Figure 16 shows average values for groups of struggling readers. But a classroom of students includes many individuals with varied history; they are not all immersed in the African American Vernacular culture, and they are not all speakers of the common form of AAVE. Some are of West Indian background; a few are African; and several are kept at home by parents who are anxious to isolate their children from the influence of street culture. Figure 17 is a scatter-

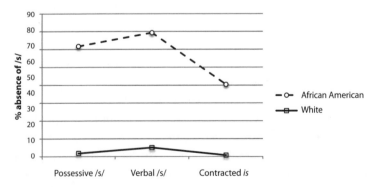

FIGURE 16. Absence of -s in the spontaneous speech of elementary school children in Philadelphia by race ($N = 287$).

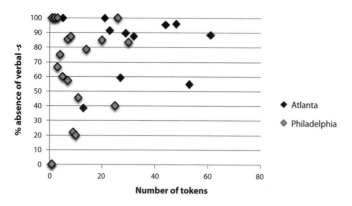

FIGURE 17. Percentage of absence of verbal -s for African American struggling readers in Philadelphia (N = 20) and Atlanta (N = 12).

gram showing the percentage of absence of verbal -s for individual African Americans by the number of occurrences of verbs where -s would be expected in Standard English.[4] Twenty are from Philadelphia and 12 from Atlanta. The number of occurrences of verbal -s for each individual varies from 1 to 61. As in any such distribution, the central tendency emerges with greater clarity as the amount of data increases.[5] It is evident that there are two such tendencies: the great majority are centered about the norm of 90% absence; the higher the number of tokens, the closer to this limiting tendency. A smaller group appear to be centered on a limit of 50%.

For the major group we can take one step further and argue that the 90% absence of verbal -s is an indication of the absence of subject-verb agreement in the underlying AAVE grammar. There are many pieces of evidence that point in this direction. In addition to the high frequency of absence on the third-person singular of the verb, we find that irregular verbs take on an invariant form: *I have, you have, he have; I do, you do, he do; I was, you was, he was, they was.* Secondly, we often find "hypercorrect" occurrences of -s on the verb in odd and unexpected places, as in (1)–(3). Thirdly, there is no tendency for the appearance or nonappearance of -s to be controlled by the phonetic context. When speakers drop a consonant or vowel that is present in their grammar, they will do so more often if its deletion makes the sequence easier to say. *Good old Mike* is likely to be pronounced *good ol'*

Mike, much more so than *good old Aaron* will be said as *good ol' Aaron.* No such tendency governs the appearance or disappearance of verbal and possessive *-s.*

If indeed the machinery of subject-verb agreement is absent in AAVE grammar, there are considerable consequences for the process of learning to read and write standard English, and as we will see, for the teachers who are trying to help children master that machinery.

This gulf between Black and White English is not limited to children's speech. The majority of African American adults in the segregated inner neighborhoods of cities like Philadelphia, New York, Los Angeles, maintain their regular use of AAVE in everyday exchanges with their family and friends. Given the high level of residential segregation throughout the United States, they satisfy Baugh's (1983) definition of users of the vernacular: people who work, play, and talk primarily with other African Americans. A limited number develop extensive cross-racial contacts, and the effect on their grammar is notable. Figure 18 shows the use of verbal *-s* for four groups of subjects in a study of North Philadelphia adults in the 1980s. The interviews with African Americans were conducted by a local African American who knew all the subjects quite well, often in groups of three or four intimate friends, so that the effect of outside observation was minimal. The majority of the speakers, those who had very little contact with whites, show 78% absence for the possessive, 72% for verbal /s/, and 52% for the copula. In contrast, the African Americans with high rates of contact with whites, and whites with high rates of contact with blacks, show very low rates of *-s* absence, and the whites with minimal black contacts, none at all.

Who were these African Americans whose grammar was so strongly shifted toward the mainstream dialect? They were not college-educated speakers who had moved out of the African American community. They remained fully accepted members of that community, and on first listening you would not detect any difference in their speech from that of the core members of the group. They included musicians who play with whites, political activists who negotiate with whites, confidence men who can "get over" whites. In the course of their daily interactions with speakers of other dialects, their underly-

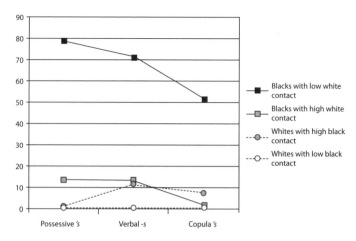

FIGURE 18. Percentage of absence of three /s/ inflections for North Philadelphia adults by race and cross-racial contacts (from Ash and Myhill 1986).

ing grammar was modified, though their use of the socially significant linguistic symbols of African American identity remained intact.

So far we have been considering only the simplest kind of grammatical fact: whether a particular element is present or absent. Studies of linguistic variation go much deeper into the matter, and explore the many ways in which the context influences this appearance or disappearance. Among the many variables of AAVE, the contraction and deletion of *is* and *are* have drawn the most attention, and the replication of these quantitative patterns displays most clearly the uniformity of AAVE throughout the United States. From our first studies of AAVE in Harlem, it appeared that the occurrence of *is*, *'s*, or zero very much depended on the grammatical form that followed. The least likelihood of a zero was found before noun phrases, as in *He a doctor;* next most likely, before an adjective, as in *He tired,* or before an indicator of place, as in *He here;* more frequently with the progressive, as in *He talkin' a lot;* and most commonly in the future, as in *He gonna go.* Figure 19 shows that this set of relations is replicated across the country in a remarkably uniform manner. The black lines and symbols show three different groups that were studied in South Harlem. The open triangles show values from Wolfram's 1969 study of Detroit

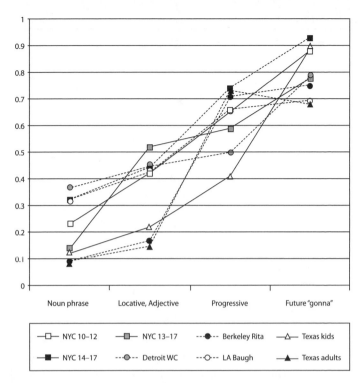

FIGURE 19. The proportion of deletion of contracted *is* by following grammatical element in eight studies of African American communities (from Rickford et al. 1991).

adolescents. The open circle reports Mitchell-Kernan's analysis of a speaker in the California Bay Area. The gray circles represent Baugh's 1983 work in Pacoima, Los Angeles. The dotted lines represent kids and adults recorded in Texas by Bailey and Cukor-Avila. There is only one small deviation from this regular pattern in all these data: the Texas adults have a slightly lower rate of absence before *gonna* in *He gonna go* than before the general progressive in *He thinkin' a lot*.

AAVE: Presence of Grammatical Elements Not Found in Other Dialects

Now let us turn to the right-hand side of figure 15: the set of particles carrying information on tense, mood, and aspect, combinations of form and meaning that are unique to AAVE. I will focus here on four of these features:

- HAD as an indicator of simple past tense
- BE as a marker of habitual aspect
- BEEN as the remote present perfect
- BE DONE as a marker of sequential tense

In the early years of AAVE studies, there was considerable disagreement about its origins, but it was generally agreed that the dialect had been more different in the past, and was now gradually converging with other dialects. In 1986 the opposite view was introduced in a series of papers based on our studies in Philadelphia (Labov and Harris 1986), and studies by G. Bailey and Maynor (1987) in Texas. We found that the differences between AAVE and other dialects were increasing. It was discovered that some of the most distinctive features of AAVE are a product of the second half of the 20th century, following the Great Migration of southern blacks to the large northern cities. Some of the most powerful evidence for this comes from the development of HAD, originally the past perfect auxiliary, as an indicator of the simple past.

HAD as a Marker of the Simple Past

Figure 20 shows a timeline, with the present moment of speaking marked, and two preceding events, A and B. Figure 20a shows that in the general grammar of English, the expressions "He pushed me; I pushed him" inform the listener that those two events occurred in that order: *first* he pushed me, *then* I pushed him. HAD before the verb operates as a marker of the past perfect, as displayed in figure 20b. The standard past perfect marker HAD is attached to the verb designating event B to indicate that it happened before A, the last event mentioned, not after it. If I say in mainstream grammar, "He pushed me; I had pushed him," the HAD marker of the past perfect tells the listener that I pushed him *before* he pushed me (as in fig. 20b). Thus the past perfect reverses the order of events that would have been understood without it, indicating that the order of statements moves backward in time.

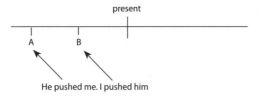

a) simple past following simple past

He pushed me. I pushed him

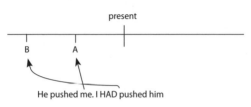

b) past perfect following simple past

He pushed me. I HAD pushed him

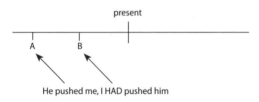

c) innovative AAVE use of HAD as a simple past

He pushed me, I HAD pushed him

FIGURE 20. The development of innovative HAD in AAVE.

Over the past five decades, AAVE has developed a use of HAD which is quite different: it marks forward movement in time like a simple preterit, as illustrated in figure 20c. Here the verb following HAD indicates an event that occurred *after* the one preceding. This is particularly common in narrative, so we can draw any number of examples from interviews with young speakers of AAVE.

(11) Tyreke, 9, telling about a dream that really scared him.
I was sleep in my brother's bed, and when they's all downstairs, my whole family's downstairs with the cake 'cuz, it's my birthday, then I HAD woke up.

Here it is clear that Tyreke woke up after he had the dream, not before it.

(12) Another dream of Tyreke's:
  It was this monster, then I HAD got the Super Nintendo, hit him with
  the head, but that didn't work, then I ran downstairs, then I woke up.

Here again, it is evident that Tyreke got the Super Nintendo after he
saw the monster in his dream, not before.

(13) Sharya, 8, talking about a fight with a girl bigger than her:
  Well, I was like, at my grandma's house, and I went back home, cuz
  my mom, me and Sabrina was here, and then I went back home. And
  I said, "Sabrina, you got a rope that we can play with Sinquetta an' em"
  and she HAD said "Yeah" so then Sinquetta and them had to go back
  in the house, la, la, la, blah, blah, blah, then some other big girl. We
  was playin' rope right, then she gon jump in and she say "You might
  jump better, and not be 'flicted."[6] I said "It's not going to be 'flicted, cuz
  I know how to turn." And then she only got up to ten. She was mad at
  me, and she HAD hit me, so I hit her right back. Sabrina jumped in it.
  And start hittin' her.

We note that in the first use of HAD, Sabrina's "Yeah" can only follow
Sharya's request, not precede it. In the second use of HAD, the big
girl got mad first, and then hit Sharya, not the other way around.

In their year-by-year studies of Springville, Texas, Cukor-Avila
(1995) and G. Bailey (1993) found that this innovative use of HAD did
not exist for Texas speakers born before World War II, and gradually
increased to 70% for those born after 1970. Figure 21 displays this
dramatic development.

Habitual BE in AAVE

A parallel development can be observed in one of the widely recognized features of AAVE, habitual BE.

(14) A: Do you know where I can find Nukey?
  B: She BE here but she isn't here now.

This form of the verb is recognized by its invariant form BE: *I be, you
be, she be,* in contrast with *I am, you are, she is.* In (14), the response of
speaker B contrasts the invariant BE of *She be here,* meaning "she is
usually here" with *She isn't (or ain't) here,* which indicates that "she

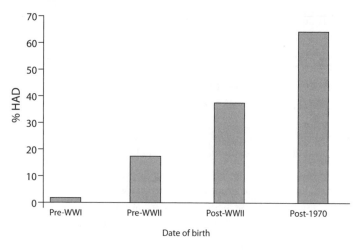

FIGURE 21. Increase in HAD + past as a simple past over time: innovative HAD as a percentage of past forms (based on Cukor-Avila 1995).

is not here right now." I will refer to the invariant form as "habitual BE." It often occurs in conjunction with the adverb *always,* but with or without an adverb it carries the meaning "this event occurs an indefinite number of times," making a distinction that is not available in the grammars of other English dialects.

Habitual BE is widespread across all forms of African American English, not limited to AAVE. Though it does occur frequently in interview materials, the full semantic impact is best shown from observations of social interaction on the street, in service encounters, and exchanges among friends. Here are examples noted by Penn students in my classes as they observed the world around them. Example (15) occurred during a game of Scrabble: Girl 1 had been making up words and trying to pass them off as real words.

(15) Girl 1: "Yea, that's a word . . ."
Girl 2: "I don't know why you BE frontin' like those are real words!"
(observed by Allison Johnson, October 7, 2005)

In (16), Penn students are observing some local guys in a pick-up game:

(16) M1: Watch! I'm 'bout to score on this play!

M2: He always think he 'bout to score. I don't know why, he ain't scored yet!

M3: Yeah, you always BE doin' that!

(observed by Matthew Williams, October 5, 2009)

Note that in AAVE, the adverb *always* precedes the verb, but in the mainstream equivalent it follows, as in "You are always doing that." Once a person becomes aware of habitual BE, they will hear themselves using it more and more often; so one of my students recorded:

(17) Me: Have you done the linguistics homework yet?

Friend: Not yet, but I BE sayin' it all the time. See! I did it right then without even thinking about it.

(observed by Jihan Thompson, October 6, 2005)

The expressive power of habitual BE is clearly shown in (18), an observation made outside McDonald's:

(18) [On the way in]

Homeless: You got any change?

Me: No. Sorry.

Homeless: A'ight, maybe when you come out.

Me: Maybe.

[After I come out]

Homeless: You got any?

[Hand him some change]

Homeless: Thank you man. People BE tellin' me when they come out they still don't have change and I KNOW they BE lyin'. Thank you.

(observed by Dan Gustafson, October 4, 2004)

At the other end of the social spectrum, (19) is an observation made at a choir practice by Elizabeth Dayton in her long-term (1996) study of AAVE grammar in Philadelphia:[7]

(19) Choir director: Will everybody remember that?

Member of the choir: Yeah but Angie, can we sing the chorus twice before we go into the other part? 'Cause it's like you BE just about to feel Jesus then we stop.

Just as in the case of innovative HAD, we observe a spectacular rise in the frequency of habitual BE. In Guy Bailey's 1993 report on Springville, Texas, we find that this use of BE was rare among those born from 1844 to 1944: only 4% of the uses of BE had this habitual meaning. For those born between 1945 and 1962, the number jumps to 52%; for the youngest generation of Springville African Americans, born between 1970 and 1976, the proportion leaps to 80%.

Remote Present Perfect BIN

We will now turn to a more complex grammatical device, remote present perfect BIN, as in example (20).

(20) She BIN married.

This BIN is strongly stressed, and pronounced with a low tone: the pitch of the voice goes down, not up.

Rickford (1975) discovered that when white listeners hear this stressed BIN, they think of it as a result of dropping the contracted auxiliary in "She's been married," that is, derived from "She has been married." He conducted an inquiry among both black and white speakers which began with the question. "She BEEN married. Is she still married?" For whites, 17 out of 25 respondents said "No," but only 2 of 25 African Americans did. For the 23 of the 25 who said, "Yes," this sentence is not related to "She has been married" but has the entirely different combination of meanings shown in (21).

(21) • This statement is true.
    • It has been true for a long time.
    • It is still true.

As with habitual BE, our best insights into the working of this grammatical feature come from observations of social interaction. In a prototypical context, one person will remark that someone else is wearing something new. In most uses of BIN, it is obvious that it cannot be derived by deletion of *have* or *has*.

(22) [At the Philadelphia 40th St. train station, two African American teenage boys]
    A: When you got them? [his sneakers]

B: Man, I BIN had these.

Note that this can't be derived from the nonexistent "I have been had these." Here the meaning is, "I own these; I've owned them for a long time; I still own them right now." In these uses of BIN there is frequently an underlying moral reprimand: "If you had been the observer you should be, you would have known this." This message is also obvious in (23).

(23) [Woman at hair salon, 25 years old]
　　　Hairdresser: OK, who's next?
　　　Woman: Me, I BIN waiting!

In (24), the speaker apologizes for the delay in information, and the indignation is directed elsewhere.

(24) Girl: How's your job going?
　　　Boy: I didn't tell you? I BIN quit that job like a month ago.
　　　Girl: Oh my god. Why?
　　　Boy: 'Cause they always be on my back about somethin'.

Example (25) shows an intimate combination of habitual BE and BIN.

(25) [Observed on the street]
　　　M1: Dog, where that party at?
　　　M2: I don't even know yet.
　　　M1: We always not BE knowing where the parties be at.
　　　M2: I know but we always end up finding them though.
　　　M1: Yea and we BE the life of the parties too.
　　　M2: I BIN told ya that.
　　　　　(observed by Kory Gedin, October 1, 2005)

BE DONE: Future Perfect and Resultative

Among the unique features of AAVE is the preverbal compound BE DONE, as in (26).[8]

(26) They BE DONE ate up all the food by the time we get there.

As it is used here, BE DONE can be translated *will have*, as in the standard English future perfect: "They will have eaten up all the food." The meaning is displayed in the timeline of figure 22, where two fu-

a) BE DONE and WILL HAVE as future perfect

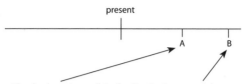

They be done ate up all the food by the time we get there
They will have eaten up all the food by the time we get there

b) BE DONE as resultative

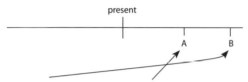

I'll be done killed that motherfucker if he tries to lay a hand on my kid again

FIGURE 22. The development of BE DONE from future perfect to resultative.

ture events, A and B, follow present time. BE DONE is attached to A, the first of these, and indicates that A will be followed by B: they will have eaten up all the food *before* we get there.

This use of BE DONE is quite common, dating back to the first studies of AAVE (Labov et al. 1968). Larry of the South Harlem Jets is quoted in (27).

(27) Cause I'll BE DONE put so many holes in him he'd a wish he hadn't said it.

Clearly, Larry would first put holes in the person who had insulted him, and then this person would regret doing so. The same ordering of events is signaled in a series of observations by Dayton in her long-term ethnographic study of tense and aspect in West Philadelphia (1993). Examples (28)–(31) were spoken by African American women in their twenties.

(28) My ice cream's gonna BE DONE melted by the time we get there.
(29) [At a vacation Bible school] They can BE DONE ate their lunch by the time they get there.

(30) I should BE DONE lost 70 pounds by the time we get there.

(31) It stink in there. You BE DONE spit up before you order.

In complex cases like (30), BE DONE is combined with other members of the auxiliary, so that a translation with "will have" is not so natural. Sometimes BE DONE is preceded by *will,* the other future marker *gonna,* or another auxiliary. But the same ordering of events holds, as also in (32), observed after a shooting in the neighborhood, when a woman was worrying about the safety of her grandchildren.

(32) I be done anoint them and pray over them before they go 'n leave out for school Monday.

(observed by Meredith Sowell, October 7, 2005)

We have hundreds of such examples of BE DONE with the interpretation of figure 22a. But another researcher found a different use of BE DONE. In the late 1970s, John Baugh was engaged in fieldwork at a swimming pool in Pacoima, a predominantly African American neighborhood of Los Angeles. It appeared that one of the lifeguards at the pool had roughed up one of the boys for alleged bad behavior. The boy's father came to the pool to deal with the situation, and Baugh heard him say (33).

(33) I'll BE DONE killed that motherfucker if he tries to lay a hand on my kid again.

This is evidently a different use of BE DONE; it cannot be an equivalent of *will have.* The translation (33') makes no sense at all:

(33') I will have killed that motherfucker if he tries to lay a hand on my kid again.

In this case, BE DONE is attached to the second of the two events, as shown in figure 22b. Baugh (1983) pointed out that AAVE had developed a new possibility of expression that is not easily translatable into mainstream dialects. This use of BE DONE can be called *resultative:* it goes beyond a simple ordering of events, but indicates that the second event will inevitably follow the first.

In the years that followed, examples with the meaning of figure 22b seem to be appearing with increasing frequency, though quantitative measures like those in figure 21 are not possible. Dayton 1996 recorded the remarkably trenchant observation from a 35-year-old woman:

(34) If you love your enemy, they BE DONE ate you alive in this society.

It would not make sense to translate it, "If you love your enemy, they will have eaten you alive in this society." *First* you love your enemy, *then* they eat you alive. The only reasonable translation is something like, "In this society, if you love your enemy it will follow as surely as the night the day that they will eat you alive." Dayton observed a number of other examples of the resultative use of BE DONE. A young black woman speaking of her nephew said:

(35) He knows best not to talk back to me 'cause I BE DONE slapped the
        little knock kneed thing upside the head.

Another girl, 17 years old, was yelling at her little cousins, ages 4, 5, and 6, who were running up and down the steps:

(36) Don't do that 'cause you BE DONE messed up your clothes!

A woman in her 20s was dealing with a barking dog:

(37) Get outta my way or I'll BE DONE slid you in the face!

If we want to generalize both types of BE DONE, we might call them *sequential,* conveying to the listener the high degree of certainty of the sequence A, B in either direction.

The four examples of grammatical features unique to AAVE demonstrate an increase in expressive power characteristic of this grammar. The examples come from social interaction involving assertions, challenges, threats, and promises, but there are also reflective generalizations like (34).

This chapter has reviewed some of the evidence that AAVE is becoming more and more different from other dialects. This divergence occurs along two dimensions: (1) African Americans participate to only a limited degree in the regional differentiation of mainstream white dialects, and (2) AAVE grammar is steadily following its own direction in the development of grammatical meanings.

Why Are Black and White Differences Increasing?

The answer to the question, why are these differences increasing? is, first and foremost, residential segregation, as reinforced and maintained by institutional racism. For most immigrant groups, residential segregation has been found to decline over time. An immigrant group arrives, settles heavily in one area, then adapts to the new country and spreads out across the whole community. Table 1, from Hershberg's 1981 study *Philadelphia: Work, Space, Family and Group Experience in the Nineteenth Century,* shows the degree of segregation by decade between 1850 and 1970. It uses the *index of dominance* to estimate segregation: that is, the proportion of a person's census tract that consists of the same group. The normal progression applies to the Irish, German, Italian, and Polish groups. For them, segregation declines in every period for which data are available. But for African Americans, the situation is radically different. Decade by decade, segregation increased until it reached a maximum in 1980.[9]

This high level of residential segregation is not peculiar to Philadelphia. In their study *American Apartheid* (1993), Massey and Denton show the index of dissimilarity—the percentage of people who would have to move to achieve total integration—for the 11 most segregated metropolitan areas: Gary, Detroit, Milwaukee, New York, Chicago, Newark, Cleveland, St. Louis, Cincinnati, Birmingham, Philadelphia.

Table 1 Indices of dominance for five ethnic groups in Philadelphia, 1850–1970

	1850	1880	1930	1940	1950	1960	1970
Black	11	12	35	45	56	72	74
Irish		34	8			5	3
German	25	11			5	3	
Italian		38			23	21	
Polish		20			9	8	

Source: Hershberg et al. 1981, table 8.

This index ranges from 87.9 (Gary, IN) to 76.9 (Philadelphia). Neither total population size nor the size of the African American community has a significant effect on this phenomenon. The New York and Chicago metropolitan statistical areas, with 11 and 10 million people, have the same level of segregation as Newark, with a little more than 2 million.

To see the linguistic implications of residential isolation, we can refer again to figure 18, which shows a great gulf between the grammatical forms used by African Americans with low degrees of white contact and those with high levels of contact with whites. Thus the effects of interaction with speakers of mainstream dialects have a strong influence on the system of grammatical suffixes. This is true even for those who continue intimate relations with core speakers of AAVE and maintain all other significant signals of membership in the AAVE community. We see this importation of mainstream grammatical signals in the speech of Walt S., a speaker classified as having a high degree of contact with whites. These contacts included various illegal activities in and out of prison. In Walt's speech, the standard grammatical signals reflected in figure 18 are not embedded in academic English. To speakers of AAVE, his speech sounds just like their own. Here is an extract from an interview with Walt that shows his use of verbal third singular -s. He is reflecting on the dangerous consequences of knowing a man who sticks up bars for a living:

(38) As a matter of fact he knows some of the people that *I* know. . . . I
was always afraid if he walked in and seen me sittin' there, he might
feel that I might give 'im up. Not that I was that type of person. . . .
Y'know what I mean, first thing he would take a look at my eyes and say
"Damn! He knows me!" Rather than take a *chance*, you know what
I mean?

This regular use of the general -s suffixes, both verbal and possessive, does not represent a wholesale switch to another dialect, but an unconscious acquisition of grammatical mechanism through contact. Walt is a thoughtful and careful speaker, but his extensive contacts with the white world have not separated him from people he has known all his life. As figure 18 shows, the musicians, political activists, con men, and hustlers whose activities reach across racial lines are distinguished linguistically from the majority of African Americans in the inner cities, users of the highly uniform AAVE grammar who have relatively little contact with speakers of other dialects. The grammatical convergence in Walt's speech shows what we might expect to find in AAVE generally if residential segregation were reduced and black children grew up with extensive interaction with speakers of other dialects. But in the present situation, the great majority of children in local schools may reach fourth grade without ever having a face-to-face conversation with speakers of mainstream dialects. They are of course bathed in standard English every day—from the mass media and from many teachers—but it is well established that this one-way form of communication has little effect on the language of those on the receiving end.[10]

In this chapter, I have tried to provide sufficient evidence to convince readers (who were not previously convinced) that AAVE is not simply a collection of deviations from standard English but a coherent and well-formed system of its own. The chapter to follow will consider the consequences of this divergence for American society.

Chapter 4 provided a view of the growing divergence of AAVE from mainstream dialects. This chapter will examine the social consequences of this divergence, and the political confusion that follows when dialect differences become a topic of public discourse.

The Black/White Gap in Reading Achievement

The high level of residential segregation in American cities is inevitably accompanied by a corresponding level of segregation in schools.[1] This leads us to look at another aspect of the division between blacks and whites in our society, the minority gap in reading achievement. Figure 23 shows the long-standing difference in reading scores for whites, blacks, and Hispanics reported by the National Assessment of Educational Progress (NAEP). There is some improvement in recent years, but the minority gap remains substantial. When we enter the fourth grade of most local schools in low-income areas, we find that a majority of the children are Below Basic on standardized tests—they do not read well enough to use reading as a tool for learning anything else—and the consequences for later learning remain throughout middle school and high school.

The earliest year tabulated in figure 23 is 1975, only a few years after the first studies of AAVE. The funding for our work in South Harlem (Labov et al. 1968) was from the Office of Education to answer the question, is there any connection between the linguistic differences involved and the gap in reading achievement? In this study, we identified and interviewed all members of the named street groups in a

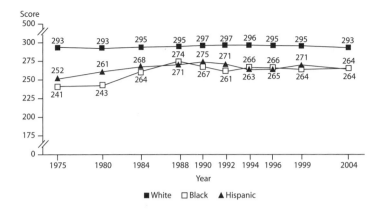

Score

FIGURE 23. The minority gap in reading achievement: average reading scores for 17-year-olds by race/ethnicity from 1975 to 2005 (National Assessment of Educational Progress).

two-block area of South Harlem—the Jets, the Cobras, the Thunderbirds, the Aces—and also interviewed a range of isolated individuals who for one reason or another did not hang out with these groups. We found the highest level of the use of AAVE features among the core members of street groups, lower levels among peripheral members, and even lower levels among the isolated individuals.

When we obtained school records of reading achievement, more dramatic differences emerged, as shown in the two sections of figure 24. Figure 24a, on the left, shows the school records for isolated individuals. Here the horizontal axis is school grade, and the vertical axis is the New York Metropolitan Achievement Test Reading score by grade. The dotted diagonal lines define reading on grade. In figure 24a, there are 3 students above grade, 8 on grade, and 21 below grade. Most of the isolated students are behind in their reading by one or two years, but there is some evidence of upward movement. Figure 24b shows similar data for 40 members of the named hangout groups and clubs in the two blocks we studied. It shows no evidence of advancement in reading beyond grade 4, with an absolute ceiling of 4.9 reading grade level through the 10th grade. The symbols with arrows indicate those who had been expelled from school. The double symbols identify speakers who we found to be unusually gifted with verbal skills, in argument, narrative, exposition, or sing-

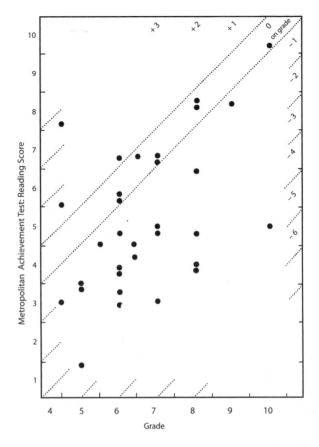

FIGURE 24a. Grade and Metropolitan Reading score for isolated individuals in south-central Harlem 1967 (from "Blacks" by Wiliam Labov in *Reading for the Disadvantaged*, edited by Thomas D. Horn, © 1970 by Harcourt Brace Jovanovitch, Inc., and reproduced with their permission).

ing. These verbally talented youth were making no more progress in reading than the others.

The differences between Figures 24a and 24b indicate that reading failure may not be a cognitive problem of language learning but rather is rooted in social behavior. Our many recordings with the street groups indicated a severe conflict between street values and the school culture which has since been well documented elsewhere (Ogbu 1982, 1987; Labov 1982a; Ferguson 2001). In our original report (Labov et al. 1968), we described substantial and systematic dif-

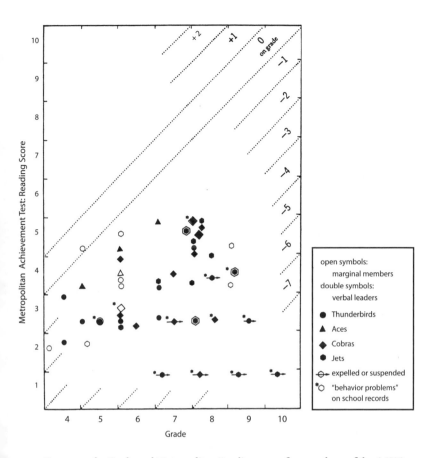

FIGURE 24b. Grade and Metropolitan Reading score for members of the AAVE street culture in south-central Harlem 1967.

ferences between AAVE and classroom English. But interference with reading was seen primarily as a result of cultural conflict: attitudes toward AAVE trigger the self-fulfilling prophecies of the "Pygmalion" effect (Rosenthal and Jacobson 1968).[2] It is not only teachers' attitudes that were involved here, but those of educational psychologists who argued that the language of black children was a series of emotional cries with no logical structure, and had to be replaced by standard English before further learning could take place.

> . . . the language of culturally deprived children . . . is not merely an underdeveloped version of standard English, but is a basically non-logical mode of expressive behavior. (Bereiter and Engelmann 1966)

The Logic of Nonstandard English

An article that I wrote entitled "The Logic of Non-standard English" (1969b) was severely critical of this point of view, and argued that AAVE (then called the Black English Vernacular) had all the capacities needed for logical thought. In the article I used an excerpt from an interview with one of the core members of the Jets, Larry Hawthorne. He was then 16 years old, one of the six best fighters in the group, a gifted storyteller, and a speaker of uncommon eloquence. The interview was conducted by our best field worker, K.C., who appeared to the Jets as an older version of themselves. Many of the youth had become involved in the Nation of Islam, and K.C. was engaging Larry in a Socratic dialogue on matters of belief, pursuing one of his favorite questions: is God black or white?

Larry: But you don't really know if it's a God or not. Nobody really knows that. Nobody!

KC: That's true. But, just saying that there is a God. What color is he? White or black?

Larry: . . . . . . He be white, man.

KC: Why?

Larry: Why? I'll tell you why. 'Cause it—the average whitey out here got everything, you dig it? an' the nigger ain't got shit, you know, you understand? so um, for then, for that to happen, you know it ain't no black God that's doin' that bullshit! . . .

KC: Yeah, I got to go for that, boy!

Larry: Dig it, that's square business, man!

The article was reprinted many times—more than anything else I have written—and an *Atlantic Monthly* version called "Academic Ignorance and Black Intelligence" was also widely disseminated (Labov 1971). It provided a platform for the voices of African American youth to be heard: the quotation from Larry alone has been reproduced many more times than the article itself. Nevertheless, this did not change the fundamental politics that determined the outcome of public discussion of the language of African Americans.

Rather than replace children's language by a new one, almost all linguists and anthropologists argue for an additive approach—giving the child the capacity to operate with both systems. To do this, it is generally agreed that contrastive analysis is helpful: putting the two systems side by side and showing the learner how they differ. Those who use contrastive analysis in the classroom generally follow this by teaching students to translate back and forth from one system to the other (LeMoine 1999; Wheeler and Swords 2006). Contrastive analysis thus depends on and develops knowledge of both systems, for both children and teachers. It is generally understood that knowledge of other groups and different cultures reduces hostility and prejudice toward them. Our sociolinguistic studies find the strongest prejudices against minority groups among those people who have had the least contact with (and the least knowledge of) them. Nevertheless, efforts to use contrastive analysis in the teaching of reading have brought forth a series of political firestorms of increasing intensity which have defeated one program after another.

The SEEK Controversy at Brooklyn College

In the year following the completion of our original research on AAVE in Harlem (Labov et al. 1968), some members of our research staff worked with Carol Reed of the SEEK (Search for Education, Elevation and Knowledge) program at Brooklyn College, with financial support from the Ford Foundation. They used the results of our linguistic studies to help prepare a contrastive analysis program for African American high school graduates whose limitations in reading and writing showed that they were not fully prepared for college. In the spring 1971 issue of the NAACP publication *The Crisis,* the SEEK program was denounced by the editor, Henry Lee Moon. His editorial, entitled "Black Nonsense," portrayed the program as a conspiracy to teach bad English to black students. In the weeks that followed, letters flowed in a steady stream from the national leaders of the civil rights movement, denouncing the SEEK program and the idea that "Black English" was anything but bad English. Bayard Rustin wrote,

"Black English" after all, has nothing to do with blackness but derives from the conditions of lower-class life in the South.

Roy Wilkins wrote in the *New York Post:*

Reinforcing this consequence of poverty will only perpetuate poverty.

Ernest McKinney, head of the Brotherhood of Sleeping Car Porters, argued:

> What is being promulgated as "Black English" is really a phenomenon out of the heads of a few white middle class "liberals" who have decided to organize Negro life and build up a body of pseudo-scholarship sometimes bordering on shysterism with the help of a few participating Negroes.

This first public firestorm also saw the beginning of a stream of mockery of poorly understood features of AAVE. Typical was a letter to *The Crisis* from Thomas W. Patrick, MD, in which it is readily apparent that the writer does not grasp the "habitual" meaning of invariant BE.

> I be suspicious. I really do be suspicious . . . I be wanting to know who will be taught Black English.

Though the Ford Foundation vigorously defended the program as a means of teaching standard English, the upshot of the controversy was that the foundation withdrew its support and (I was told informally) resolved not to become involved again in any future program that dealt with "Black English." As far as I know, they have kept their word.

The same political reaction to the recognition of AAVE by the school system can be observed in a series of controversies that followed. In case after case, efforts to use linguistic knowledge of AAVE for contrastive analysis were reported and condemned as programs for teaching children to speak a corrupt brand of English. The idea that African American children spoke a coherent dialect of their own was consistently rejected; as in the SEEK controversy, the speech differences involved were called "bad English," "slang," "ignorant and careless speech."

The Ann Arbor Trial

In the 1960s the town of Ann Arbor constructed a low-income housing project in an upper middle class area, and a number of African American children were enrolled in the Martin Luther King Elementary School there. In 1976 suit was brought against the Ann Arbor Board of Education in federal court by a group of African American mothers for the board's failure to teach their children to read, under federal statute 1702(f):

> No state shall deny equal educational opportunity to an individual on account of his or her race, color, sex or national origin by . . . (f) the failure by an educational agency to take appropriate action to overcome linguistic barriers that impede equal participation by its students in its instructional programs. (Title 20 of the U.S. Code, Section 1702)

In this case, the burden on the plaintiffs was to demonstrate the existence of a linguistic barrier. Geneva Smitherman, of Wayne State University, presented 184 extracts from recordings made in the children's homes, and mobilized a team of linguists to testify on the significance of these data, comparing them with studies of AAVE in other cities.[3]

Judge Charles Joiner found for the plaintiffs, and issued a decision in which he summed up the linguistic evidence as follows:

> All of the distinguished researchers and professionals testified as to the existence of a language system, which is a part of the English language but different in significant respects from the standard English used in the school setting, the commercial world, the world of the arts and science, among the professions, and in government. It is and has been used at some time by 80 percent of the black people of this country and has as its genesis the transactional or pidgin language of the slaves, which after a generation or two became a Creole language. Since then it has constantly been refined and brought closer to the mainstream of society. It still flourishes in areas where there are concentrations of black people. It contains aspects of Southern dialect and is used largely by black people in their casual conversation and informal talk.

Judge Joiner concluded that the home language of these children was a distinctly different dialect, and instructed the school board to provide teachers with more knowledge about this dialect (Joiner 1979, 14).

It would be difficult to improve on this summary of the linguistic consensus at that time. The statement that this language was being "refined and brought closer to the mainstream" did represent a consensus. It was 10 years before the discovery of the new evidence, presented in chapter 4, that showed that AAVE was not converging with other dialects but in many respects becoming more different.

The after-school program developed by the school board under the judge's order was not shown to be effective in raising reading levels, though it modified some teachers' views of the children's language. The case did provide a legal background for some of the efforts to introduce AAVE into the classroom 20 years later, to be discussed below. However, it also had negative repercussions, the result of many national reports in the press and radio that a federal judge had instructed teachers to learn to speak "Black English" so that they could communicate with their students. The *Dallas Morning News* published an editorial on July 16, 1979, even before the decision was published:

> Presumably seeking to encourage racial pride, blacks filed in Michigan to have the courts force the teaching of so-called "black English" for young blacks. The idea, in other words, is to have the schools not only recognize the patois of the ghetto as correct, but certify it as a separate language for black students.
>
> This is probably the worst idea since slavery, and its evil effects, if it were adopted, would cripple blacks not for years but for generations.

This produced a wave of moral indignation in which, once again, AAVE was identified with slang and with careless, ignorant, and boisterous behavior. The normally thoughtful Carl Rowan wrote:

> For a court to say that "black English" is a "foreign tongue" and require schools in Ann Arbor, Mich., or any place else to teach ghetto children in "black English" would be a tragedy. . . . What black children need is an end to this malarkey that tells them they can fail to learn grammar . . . and embrace the mumbo-jumbo of ignorance.

In the *Philadelphia Daily News* of October 12, 1979, African American columnist Chuck Stone responded to Judge Joiner with a piece headed "Black English Be Bad; Teaching It Is Worse":

> "Black English" is neither dialect nor language.
> It is a people's cognitive surrender to sloth.

It's bad pronunciation, worse grammar and the worst method of speaking.

It is the dismal inheritance from lazy-minded parents who don't care enough about their children to insist that they talk with precision. . . .

I was told that in response to these reports, the West Philadelphia school district banned the use of the Language Experience method, in which children tell stories in their own words and afterward read them back, since this would allow the use of nonstandard speech in the classroom.

The Ebonics Controversy

The most violent of these linguistic controversies, one that still reverberates in the American psyche, was the response to the "Ebonics" program of the Oakland, California, school board. The board's original resolution of December 18, 1996, contained nine paragraphs headed WHEREAS and six resolutions. The ones that drew the most public attention were:

WHEREAS, numerous validated scholarly studies demonstrate that African-American students as a part of their culture and history as African people possess and utilize a language described in various scholarly approaches as "Ebonics" (literally "Black sounds") or "Pan-African Communication Behavior" or "African Language Systems"; and

WHEREAS, these studies have also demonstrated that African Language Systems are genetically based and not a dialect of English; and . . .

WHEREAS, the Federal Bilingual Education Act (20 U.S.C. 1402 et seq.) mandates that local educational agencies "build their capacities to establish, implement and sustain programs of instruction for children and youth of limited English proficiency; and . . .

NOW, THEREFORE, BE IT

RESOLVED that the Board of Education officially recognizes the existence, and the cultural and historic bases of West and Niger-Congo African Language Systems, and each language as the predominantly primary language of African-American students; and . . .

BE IT FURTHER RESOLVED that the Superintendent in conjunction with her staff shall immediately devise and implement the best possible academic program for imparting instruction to African-American students in their primary language for the combined purposes of maintaining the legitimacy and richness of such language whether it is known as "Ebonics," "African Language Systems," "Pan-African Communication Behaviors" or other description, and to facilitate their acquisition and mastery of English language skills. . . .

The cry of outrage which this proposal evoked has not yet subsided. It is evident that the Oakland resolution went far beyond the proposals for contrastive analysis of the SEEK program or the Ann Arbor decision (cited indirectly in the third WHEREAS above). People understandably read this resolution as asserting that African Americans spoke a completely different language (and therefore did not speak English), that this was an African language (like Yoruba, Fante, Twi), that it was genetically inherited, and that instruction in the classroom had to be conducted in that language. In the days that followed, many national African American leaders condemned the resolution. The Reverend Jesse Jackson said,

> While we are fighting in California trying to extend affirmative action and fighting to teach our children so they become more qualified for jobs, in Oakland some madness has erupted over making slang talk a second language. You don't have to go to school to learn to talk garbage.

The Oakland school board issued some amendments and clarification. The word "genetically" was explained as meaning "historically." It was emphasized that the program as a whole was designed to help students read and write Standard English.[4] But as in the Ann Arbor case, this account was regularly reversed when it was reported in the media. The *Times-Picayune* of New Orleans ran a headline: "Oakland to teach 'Black English.'" The *Sacramento Bee* headlined: "Oakland Schools OK Teaching of Black Dialect."

Both political and academic figures responded to the Oakland program with the extreme rhetoric that was first heard from Jesse Jackson. The governor of California's press secretary, Sean Walsh, issued a statement:

> The mainstreaming of this ridiculous theory will only serve to hold [disadvantaged children] back. We have no interest at the state level of encouraging this highly dubious plan.

Walter B. Williams of George Mason University wrote,

> The bottom line is so-called black English is nonsense and attempted
> cover-up of government school corruption and capitulation to mediocrity.[5]

In contrast, many linguists rallied to the support of the Oakland
school board, although the language of the resolution was quite remote from the linguistic point of view. The term "Ebonics" was
originally created by the psychologist Robert Williams and adopted
by Ernest Smith for the use reflected in the Oakland school board
resolution. No other linguist uses it to describe the dialect of African
Americans, as far as I know, nor do they follow the claims for an African structure of AAVE. Linguists did support the general concept that
knowledge of children's home dialect was essential for the effective
teaching of standard English. A resolution written by John Rickford
was unanimously adopted by the Linguistic Society of America. It
centered on two fundamental points:

> All human linguistic systems—spoken, signed, and written—are funda-
> mentally regular.
>
> The distinction between "languages" and "dialects" is usually made
> more on social and political grounds than on purely linguistic ones.

The tremendous outpouring of public sentiment against "Ebonics" involved two themes that are deeply rooted in popular views of
language and altogether contrary to the linguistic point of view.

(1) *Talking about something teaches it.* The impression that the Oakland
    school board was teaching Black English was based on the belief that
    any introduction of a nonstandard dialect into the classroom instructs
    children to use that form of language in speaking and writing.

(2) *A language is its words.* The repeated insistence that Black English was
    nothing but the use of bad words like *ain't* rests on the view that a
    language is primarily a vocabulary, rather than rules for the use of those
    words. For most letter writers, bloggers, and reporters, the distinctive
    character of Ebonics, Black English, or AAVE is the unconstrained use
    of slang and the absence of any rules of grammar.

However, one grammatical feature of AAVE was and is prominent in
public discourse: the use of habitual BE. Chuck Stone continued his
diatribe against Black English:

And "be" is used as if it were an active verb instead of an auxiliary verb. ... The terribly abused "be" ought to be banned for five years in the black community.

Almost every description or imagined projection of Ebonics features a use of invariant BE. We read in "THE OFFICIAL EBONICS GUIDE to help whitey translate the negroid-american language into standard English":

The negroid mind has a common problem with conjugating the verb "to be," so they continue to refer to everything as "be." I be, You be, She/He/It be, We be, They be.[6]

Here is a definition of Ebonics found on the Internet:

A "variation" of English entirely made up of slang and southern word shortenings. It is generally spoken in the "hood" (neighborhood) and has almost no defined syntactical structure. Also of note is the almost complete lack of conjugation of verbs ("I be", "she be", "thems be", etc) and the mixing of pronouns. When spoken in any educated circles, its usage usually screams "I am illiterate."[7]

The gap between the popular impression of AAVE and the linguistic reality is clear in the public use of BE. The casual observer notes that BE is invariant: it is used where other dialects show *is* or *are*. But the semantic content of BE as "habitual" is not observed, and the great majority of these "Ebonic" creations are starkly ungrammatical, as in the joke delivered by Bill Cosby:

Q: Do you know what "Toys-R-Us" is called in Harlem?
A: We Be Toys.

Misperception of AAVE grammar is omnipresent in public discussion. An advertisement was run in the *New York Times* on behalf of "Atlanta Black Professionals" showing an image of Martin Luther King delivering a speech that begins, "I has a dream." The ad warned of the dire consequences of young black people speaking Ebonics, which would prevent them from gaining access to the soaring rhetoric of Dr. King. But the writers of the ad were so remote from the reality of daily life that they did not realize that their specimen sentence could never be spoken. As noted in chapter 4, AAVE regularly uses *do*, not *does; was* not *were;* and *have*, not *has*. "I have a dream" is the only possible form in AAVE as well as in Standard English.[8]

It would be difficult to overestimate the degree of hostility toward "Ebonics" and "Black English" in public discussion. No particular feature of language need be mentioned. A typical definition of Ebonics is found on urbandictionary.com and widely copied:

> A poor excuse for a failure to grasp the basics of english. When in doubt, throw an "izzle" sound in the middle of any word or just string random thoughts together and insinuate that they actually mean something. When backed into a corner, you can always claim that it has something to do with a sort of symbolism or is a defining trait that makes your race great, versus own up to the fact that it is essentially laziness at it's [*sic*] finest.

Teachers generally share this uninformed and hostile view of African American children's language. A common reaction of teachers to children's speech is to reject it as not a form of language at all. Thus we typically hear:

Fourth grade student in Davis School (about the wrestling match he went to): They be slammin' them all over the place.
Teacher: Speak English!

The rejection of the child's language is only one of the many aspects of the educational system that leads to alienation and discouragement in the early grades.

Ebonics Humor

The most aggressive expression of this hostility is found in the large volume of humor directed at Ebonics and Black English.[9] We have "Onics" jokes such as

Eskimo-American speak	Harpoonics
Italo-American Speak	Rigatonics
Oakland-school-board Speak	Moronics

Many such jokes are plainly and simply expressions of hostility toward blacks, as in this Ebonics definition of OMELETTE:

Every time I start a new job, OMELETTE go after a week.

In the following definition of AFRO, the same author shows that he thinks that African Americans say "frow" for "throw." He does not realize that in AAVE *th* at the beginning of a word is never pronounced /f/, but only in syllable final position.

AFRO—I got so mad at my bitch, AFRO a lamp at her.

At Ivy League schools Vassar and Cornell, comic treatments of Ebonics appeared in college newspapers. In the *Cornell Review*'s parody "Course Descriptions for the Africana Major," the course on racism was described as "Da White Man be evil an he tryin to keep da brotherman down." To give the students credit, it should be noted that there was a considerable backlash: 200 copies of the paper were publicly burned.

Here are extracts from "Ebonic Olympic games":

Track and field
    Rob, Shoot & Run
    9 MM Pistol Toss
    Molotov Cocktail Throw
    Bitch-slapping (Bruises inflicted on wife/girlfriend in three one-minute rounds)
Ebo-Decathlon
    Rob Liquor Store
    Guzzle One-Fifth of Fortified Wine
    Drink Six-Pack of Old English 800
    Steal One BMW
    Have Sex with Prostitute
    Pimp Girlfriend to Family Member . . .
    Sponsors: ACLU, Oakland Board of Education, Congress, and the Supreme Court

Rickford and A. E. Rickford eloquently sum up the meaning and social impact of this strain of public reaction to Ebonics:

For those behind this most virulent strain of Ebonics Humor, Ebonics was never a language. Or a dialect. Or an educational policy. Or a matter of public outrage. For bigots, Ebonics simply served as a metaphor for their stereotypes of African Americans—as criminals and crackheads and welfare defrauders and liars and gangbangers. . . . Because everyone supposedly agreed that Ebonics was ludicrous and laughable one could use the consensus as a cover for much darker kinds of humor. . . . In short, "Ebonics" became a new "slur," a "nigger" upon whom one could inflict a Rodney-King type beating while wearing the helmet of "wit." (1976, 218)

Waves of reaction against Black English continue with predictable regularity. As recently as March 10, 2010, a controversy erupted at the University of North Carolina–Wilmington over a course taught by Maurice Martínez, a professor of secondary education who has included Black English as part of his curriculum.[10] Mike Adams, a disgruntled professor of criminology and right-wing blogger, campaigned to have students' tuition for Dr. Martinez's classes refunded. Among his objections we read:

Maurice, the tenured education professor, also informs students that when using plurals it is not necessary to add an "s" in Black English. That's why a paper costs "50 cent," not "50 cents." Is this making sense? Or do we say "making cent"?

Here again one can see the distance between public discussion and linguistic reality. The absence of /s/ in "50 cent" is a general feature of Southern English specifically limited to "nouns of measure" like "cent, dollar, pound." (McDavid and McDavid 1964). The ungrammatical extension to "making cent" is one more example of an uninformed reaction masquerading under "the helmet of 'wit.'"

Dialect Readers

Another way in which knowledge of AAVE was put to use in the classroom was in the creation of dialect readers. In 1976 Houghton-Mifflin launched Bridge: A Cross-Cultural Reading Program, by Gary Simpkins, Grace Holt, and Charlesetta Simpkins (1977). The program was introduced to its users by the program's spokesman, the recorded voice of a young African American:

What's happenin', brothers and sisters? I want to tell you about this here program called *Bridge*, a cross-cultural reading program. Now I *know* what you thinkin'. This is just another one of them jive reading programs, and that I won't be needin' no readin' program. But dig it. This here reading program is really kinda different. It was done by a brother and two sisters, soul folk, you know. And they put sump'm extra in it, they put a little taste o' soul. Matter of fact, a lot of soul. . . . Now I *know* what you gon' say. I don' need to be readin' no better, I get by! I don't *dig* no readin'. And they ain't nothin' I want to be readin' nohow. But dig! I know where you *been*, and I know where you comin' from too. When you was jus' startin' in school, readin' got on yo' case, now didn't it, got down on you, hurt your feelings. In the second grade, readin' jus' smacked you all upside yo' head, dared you do sump'm about it. In the third grade, hum, readin' got into your ches', knocked you down, dragged you through the *mud*, sent you home cryin' to yo' mama. Now, by the time you got to the fo'th grade, you jus' about had enough of messin' around with this here readin' thing. And you said to yourself, I ain' gon' be messin' with this ol' bad boy no *more*! You jus' hung it up. . . . So anyway, you stopped tryin', so you was just sick and tired of gittin' done in, bein' bored all the time by that readin' stuff. But dig! like I said now, this here program is kind of different. I want to hip you to that. It can help you git it together. . . . And it ain't *borin'*. Cause it's about really interesting people. Matter of fact, it's about the most interesting people in the world, black people, and you know how interesting bloods can be.

Forty years after, this introduction sounds quaint and produces laughter from African American college students. Its outmoded expressions underline the problems of using current idiom in textbooks. But at the time, Bridge was powerful and effective. The spokesman described precisely the situation of the majority of children in the inner-city fourth grades of Harlem, Philadelphia, Atlanta, and Los Angeles. In appealing directly to them, Bridge bypassed the institutional bias that makes young black children feel that they and their language are irrelevant to the educational program.

The initial readings were in the authors' versions of AAVE, and dealt with African American themes and folklore. Bridge was tested in five areas of the United States, with 14 teachers and 27 classes from the 7th through the 12th grades, involving 540 students—all but 10 of them black. The 21 classes that used the Bridge program showed a significantly larger gain in reading than the 6 control classes: an average gain of 6.2 months for 4 months of instruction as compared to 1.6 months for the control group (Simpkins and Simpkins 1981). On the basis of this impressive finding, the program was marketed nationally by Houghton-Mifflin.

The wave of reaction against the use of Black English in the classroom did not spare Bridge. The publishers received enough objections from parents and teachers that they ceased promoting it, and further development was shelved.[11]

The Reading Road and Portals to Reading

Until 1995, my efforts to understand the impact of Black English on reading were carried on outside the school system. The view of the classroom reflected in figure 24 was the product of these community studies, which also recorded the resentment of and alienation from school ideology by the main body of African American youth in Harlem. But I still hoped that this knowledge could be used to close the minority gap in reading, and in 1996 I agreed to join the National Research Council Committee on Preventing Reading Difficulties Among Young Children, where I began to learn the fundamentals of reading research. Over the next two years I grasped several generalizations as they emerged from the committee discussion and were finally published in the committee report (Snow, Burns, and Griffin 1998).

(1) One cannot bypass the alphabet in the teaching of reading. Phonemic awareness and knowledge of graphemic/phonemic relations are strongly correlated with reading achievement. They are not acquired automatically but must be taught explicitly to most children.

(2) Changing attitudes, raising self-esteem, and creating warm rapport with children do not in themselves raise reading scores.

(3) None of the methods for the teaching of reading available at that time were effective in closing the minority gap in reading.

On January 23, 1997, Senator Arlen Specter convened a hearing of the Senate Subcommittee on Labor, Health, Human Services, and

Education on the topic of Ebonics. Members of the Oakland school board, an Oakland high school senior, the psychologist Robert Williams, and several linguists (including myself) testified in support of the Oakland program. An African American minister from Kansas and a conservative African American radio talk show host were highly critical of Ebonics. At the end of the session, Senator Specter asked me, "What reason do we have to think that using knowledge of Black English will improve reading?" I answered, "We don't know, because every effort to find out has been interrupted before it was done." Senator Specter then inserted language into an appropriations bill which assigned $1 million to the University of Pennsylvania for research on reading. I developed a research program in partnership with the Oakland school board and California State University–Hayward to develop the answer to the question posed by Specter. Two-thirds of the funds were assigned to the California group, which did not pursue actual methods of teaching reading but focused instead on the professional development of teachers. At Penn, we developed an Individualized Reading Program for the use of undergraduates in service-learning courses on Black English. In these courses, students learn the basic patterns of AAVE and its history as presented in chapter 4, and use that knowledge to tutor elementary school children in local schools.

From 2001 to 2005 this program was tested on a national scale with funds from NSF, NIH, the Office of Education, and the Spencer Foundation. Over a thousand students were tutored in Philadelphia, Atlanta, and Northern and Southern California. In the years that followed, the tutoring program was further developed as The Reading Road and is now the main instrument of a student-run project, the Penn Reading Initiative (http://pri.sas.upenn.edu), at the University of Pennsylvania and at several other universities.

The Reading Road builds on three research findings:

(1) Most struggling readers have actually mastered the alphabetic principle as far as the basic relations between sound and spelling are concerned. Their errors are concentrated on combinatory problems where several letters combine to signal one sound or one letter signals more than one sound.

(2) Many apparent errors in oral reading are actually differences in pronunciation between AAVE and Standard English.

(3) Alienated and discouraged readers find the acquisition of literacy irrelevant to the problems that they have to deal with in everyday life.

The Reading Road attacks these three problems by direct instruction on combinatory problems, by instructing tutors on the pronunciation patterns of AAVE, and by reading materials that engage the emotional and social concerns of minority students in low-income schools.

As one way of reaching larger populations of struggling readers, I incorporated the basic approach of The Reading Road into a commercial intervention program. Portals to Reading is a full language-arts series for grades 4–8, published by Houghton-Mifflin Harcourt and now being marketed in California and Texas. It is centered on 32 short "graphic novels," some new, some based on the stories of The Reading Road. They all follow the three imperatives of The Reading Road—to develop alphabetic knowledge, to take into account children's home language, and to deal with the central conflicts of children's everyday life.

Each chapter of this approach to reading begins with instruction on a particular alphabetic combination. The texts of the graphic novels are written so that 75% of the words follow phonics rules taught in this and preceding chapters. Here we use linguistic knowledge of how letters of the alphabet combine to stand for particular sounds and meanings, like the silent-e rule that distinguishes *hate* from *hat*, or the final combinations *-ld*, *-nd*, *-sp*, *-sps*. We add to this our knowledge of how AAVE may differ from classroom English in the realization of these combinations in speech. A key example is the word *wasps*. We know that the *-sps* cluster is rarely pronounced as it is written. Our emphasis is on decoding *wasps* as the plural of *wasp*, rather than drilling on a pronunciation pattern that is beyond the reach of many adults as well as children.

The driving force behind The Reading Road and Portals is not the direct instruction but the use of what is learned in reading the graphic novels that follow. In one such story, "Ghosts in the Basement," a 10-year-old boy reluctantly follows his sister down into their dark basement, where he sees something gray and fuzzy and hits it with a stick.

> I screamed, "Tamara! I just killed a ghost!" Tamara came up. "That's no ghost. That's a wasps' nest." I said, "It's not wasps! It's a ghost's nest." Tamara said, "It isn't a ghost. It's a wasps' nest. There were wasps down here last spring. And they stung me too!"

Here a political issue in teaching reading comes to the fore. Do we halt the reading program to develop new skills in pronunciation, or do we focus on recognizing the meanings of the words? The approach taken in Portals recognizes that different teachers will come down on either side of the question. The teacher's edition includes for each graphic novel a letter on professional development addressed to teachers written and signed by me. The page on "Ghosts in the Basement" calls attention to the fact that this passage deals with the most difficult combinations of three consonants, at the beginnings and ends of words, *ghost's nests* and *wasps' nests*. For many speakers of English, the -*sts*, -*sps*, and -*sks* combinations are a formidable obstacle. Even with much effort, *tests* is pronounced as *tesses*, or *testes*, or simply *tesss*, with a long *s*. This applies to speakers of Appalachian English as well as speakers of AAVE, and many speakers of mainstream dialects besides. It is up to the teachers to decide how much emphasis they want to place on pronunciation and how much on reading. They may take the route, "Learn to say it, and then to read it." Or decide, "Learn to read it, and practice your pronunciation some other time."

Teaching the Possessive to Speakers of AAVE

A crucial question asked in our research was whether there was a correlation between reading errors and the students' use of AAVE features in speech. Table 2 shows that there is such a correlation—not large, but a significant one. The pre-test and post-test figures are taken from our RX test, a measure of the child's knowledge of sound-to-letter correspondences in decoding a standard reading of 555 words. Before instruction, there are significant correlations between the absence of verbal /s/, absence of possessive /s/, and absence of copula /s/ and the mean error rate on the RX test. After 24 to 40 hours of instruction, only the correlation with the copula remains.

Table 2 Correlation of AAVE variables in spontaneous speech with reading errors in pre- and post-test of The Reading Road, 2001–2

	Pre-instruction test		Post-instruction test	
	r-corr.	prob.	r-corr.	prob.
Absence of verbal /s/	.177	.0012	.06	n.s.
Absence of possessive /s/	.137	.013	.086	n.s.
Absence of copula /s/	.221	<.00001	.239	<.00001

Note: N = 287

An unexpected effect of reading the possessive -s appeared in research on African American children's development at the University of North Carolina (Terry et al. 2010). Seventy-five second graders were tested with a wide variety of linguistic and cognitive measures. Scores were obtained on the Calculation and Applied Subtests of the Woodcock-Johnson R-battery. The frequency of verbal -s and possessive -s suffixes in the texts of the word problems was found to interfere significantly with success in doing the computations.[12]

We are still far from understanding the ways in which dialect differences interfere with reading. But one clear example can be found in the contrast between standard *whose* and AAVE *who*. The standard English sentence *I don't know whose book it was* is regularly heard in AAVE as *I don't know who book it was*. In other words, *whose* is treated as if it were spelled *who's* and the *'s* is dropped. Our RX post-instruction test is a story about a bad-tempered cat that won't come out of a tree, gets knocked off, and lands on its owner's head. The ending reads:

> The cat landed on Ray's head and dug its claws in Ray's nose
> Ray was screaming, "Get off my head!"
> The cat wouldn't listen but just kept digging instead
> He took off wearing that cat for a hat
> It wasn't very pretty but whose fault was that
> Not mine I thought as Ray ran down the street
> That would be the last time that all of us would meet

Faced with the problem of recognizing and interpreting the /s/ in *whose,* many speakers of AAVE choose the nearest common word ending in /s/: *was.* Once they do this, the next word *fault* becomes even more difficult to identify than its complex spelling would predict. We then find five examples of African American readers in California struggling with the problem:

Text: It wasn't very pretty but	whose	fault	was that
C-03 (2nd grade):	was	float	was that
C-04 (2nd grade):	was	fell	was that
C-07 (3rd grade):	was	frote	was that
C-27 (4th grade):	was	full	was that
C-23 (3rd grade):	wasn't	fight	was that

However, C-32 (2nd grade) read *whose* correctly (with the correct meaning) as *who,* and then self-corrected *fell* to *fault.* C-37 read *who,* corrected it to *whose,* and then self-corrected *felt* to *fault:*

C-32 (2nd grade):	who	fell -> fault was that
C-37 (4th grade):	who -> whose	felt -> fault was that

In California, 17% of African American students read *was* for *whose,* but only 7% of the white readers did this. The conclusion we come to is that the possessive suffix in *whose* is an impediment to decoding and reading comprehension.

The Reading Road attacks the problem of the possessive with a narrative "Whose Dollar Is It?" In this story, the protagonist is given a dollar by a friend who asks him to keep quiet about it for reasons that will appear later. But the dollar falls out of the narrator's book in front of Mr. Benson, the English teacher.

Mr. Benson said, "Is that your dollar?"
I said, "No, it isn't."
He said, "Whose dollar is it?"
I said, "I don't know whose dollar it is."
He said, "Janine told me that she lost a dollar this morning. Is that her dollar?"
I said, "No, it isn't."

He said, "If you know it isn't Janine's dollar, then you know whose dollar it is."

I said, "No, I don't.

Knowing that *whose* is an alien element in the grammar of most of our readers, we give intensive practice, not just in decoding, but in figuring out just what it means and what translation is needed to derive the right meaning.

This is only possible if we recognize the difference between dialect differences and incorrect interpretation of what is on the printed page. Thus we will need teachers and tutors to recognize that if a child reads "I don't know who dollar it is," he or she has correctly deciphered the meaning of the text. But here we return to the difference between the general, popular view of AAVE and the linguistic reality.

What Language to Use?

At the outset, a primary question had to be addressed: What kind of language would appear in these stories? Black English, Standard English, or something in between? The decision was a political one, motivated by the history, reviewed earlier in this chapter, of defeated efforts to introduce Black English into the classroom—in contrastive analysis or in dialect readers. The politics of the national controversies over AAVE were echoed in the behavior of teachers and principals in local schools. The most common reaction of teachers to nonstandard English—even a single "ain't"—is negative in the extreme.

Here we have to draw a sharp distinction between two different uses of AAVE in the classroom. One is teaching *about* AAVE, and other nonstandard dialects. This can be done as part of a general educational program to teach respect and appreciation of language variation (Reaser and Wolfram 2006; Hudley and Mallinson 2011). The other is *reading and writing in AAVE* as a means of acquiring basic skills. The political objections that have been raised center on the second use, and misinterpretations of the first. The underlying problem seems to spring from the belief that any use of language as a medium of instruction implies that the school as an institution is endorsing and approving that language. Given the history of efforts to bring contrastive analysis into the classroom, it seems that a successful program must be accompanied by a vigorous effort to inform school administrators and parents about its nature and goals.

The use of contrastive analysis in the classroom is usually more than an effort to improve attitudes. It would involve systematic teaching of differences in rule systems as a means of acquiring bidialectal competence, making students fully conscious of the rules that govern their own speech and giving them practice in rapid code switching (Wheeler and Swords 2006). Whether or not this can be done without triggering the interpretation that students are being *taught* AAVE is a subtle and difficult question.

The political problem of satisfying educators' expectations extends beyond language to issues of story content. "No Pets on the Bus" is about a boy who gets onto the school bus with a box holding a rat named Bip. A notice on the bus reads "No Pets on the Bus," and kids on the bus get into a fierce argument as to whether a rat is a pet or not. The part of Bip is a popular one: third graders competed with each other for the right to read Bip, who talks only in nonsense syllables like "Wik wik," "Nik nik," and "Vik vik." A West Coast principal who saw an early version of this story objected to the rat. He said, "What if some child actually *had* a rat in his house? He would be very upset." Judging from my own experience, this would in fact increase the interest of the story for that child. But in this case I followed the general principle: battles that are fought in the classroom are usually lost in the classroom. It was not an easy problem, because the animal had to be one whose status as a pet could be disputed. A pet bat was rejected because some bats have rabies, and it was feared that a child might try to keep a bat as a pet after reading the story. Finally, in the Portals version, the pet rat morphed into a pet pig, who in the hands of our illustrators was even more appealing.

Weighing the force of teachers' reactions from a sociolinguistic perspective, we came to the conclusion that the grammar of the protagonists of our narratives, no matter how fiercely they might struggle against institutional authority, had to be standard. The battle for the recognition of AAVE in the classroom, begun in "The Logic of Nonstandard English" (1969b), might be won, but it would be a long and expensive battle, waged at the expense of children who could have learned to read under a more realistic approach. The approach that has been taken in The Reading Road and Portals is to provide contrastive analysis for teachers rather than for students.

The protagonists of our narratives speak grammatically in the Standard English sense, but this does not mean that they speak properly. They use the idiom of everyday life in the black community—but not in a form that teachers would recognize as slang or nonstandard. In The Reading Road, someone doesn't ask to "borrow" a dollar, he asks to "hold" a dollar. In "Dealing with Zeke," a mother warns her son, who has been suspended for fighting once too often:

> My mom used to say, "Boy, don't play the fool
> You know I work all day so you need to be in school."

This is not nonstandard English, but neither is it the proper language of the classroom. A story called "On the Phone" focuses on words with digraphs *ph, sh, ch*. Sheila is telling the story of how she got in trouble for copying a wrong answer in a geography test by copying from Shanetta's paper:

> Shanetta came up to me and said, "Sheila you cheated on the geography test." Can you believe that? Now you know I just can't do geography . . . Anyhow, I told her, "Shut your mouth, girl! You had no business putting the wrong thing on your answer sheet, so I had to see it!" And I don't know why she got all mad, because what I said was just common sense. And she went to push me.

The technical term for what we are trying to achieve is "high text-to-self realization." It is the language that we hear every day, drenched in tones of moral indignation, the voice of those who feel that the world is stacked against them, continually blamed for things they did not do, as well as for the things that they did. We therefore seek a political alignment with struggling readers, as a means of engaging them in the reading process.

One can detect in these extracts an underlying principle that drives our approach: "Nice is not interesting." Inspecting the materials that our students are given to read in the regular classroom, we find that they are nice, and not interesting. Whether we like it or not, the world of everyday speech is driven by conflict and by the indignation that leads many of our struggling readers to behave like bad little kids. In our tutoring program we lose more than a few students suspended for fighting. We do not deny the need for them to behave like good little kids if they are going to succeed in school. But we do not believe that it is necessary for them to become good little kids before they can begin to read.

We also recognize that conflicts among kids have to be settled without violence if our students are to continue in school and achieve educational success. The stories in our reading program are therefore studded with instances of conflict resolved by verbal means which we hope will be useful models toward that end.

The Students' View of the World

We have come a long way from the 1960s in terms of civil rights, but the minority gap in reading does not show much improvement. President Obama's 2009 speech to the NAACP laid out a number of educational programs that he hopes will serve, in his words, "to overcome the inequities, the injustices and the barriers that still exist in our system." He then turned to address African American youth directly:

> Yes, if you're African American, the odds of growing up among crimes and gangs are high. Yes, if you live in a poor neighborhood you will face challenges that somebody in a wealthy suburb does not have to face.
>
> But that's not a reason to get bad grades.
>
> That's not a reason to cut classes.
>
> That's not a reason to give up on your education and drop out of school. . . .
>
> That's what we have to teach all of our children: No excuses!
> (Address to NAACP, July 16, 2009)

In order to realize this message in low-income schools, we have to understand as much as we can of the reasons for the discouragement and alienation that dominate the classroom from the third grade on. To give some view of the size and depth of the problem, I will draw upon our recent interviews with struggling readers to let their voice and their point of view be heard.

To learn more about the language and experience of the children involved, over 500 were interviewed and recorded in the 2nd, 3rd, and 4th grades. The interviewing techniques were based on the sociolinguistic studies developed over the years to record the vernacular of everyday life, drawing upon personal experiences with the greatest emotional impact.

Latasha, from West Philadelphia, is one of the many hundreds who spoke freely on these topics. She is archetypical of the young, intelligent student who is getting deeper and deeper into trouble with the school system. In the second grade, she is due to get an F in behavior. She is also typical of the many children we tutor who are suspended (and expelled) for fighting. In answer to the question, "Did you ever get blamed for something you didn't do?" she said:

> Well . . . well I used to be bad—I used to be bad in first grade and kindergarten. But—and then when they come to second grade and stuff they always blame me stuff cuz they know I always do that but I always be good in second grade. I—but I used to be bad in first and kindergarten cuz it wasn't really nothing to do, so I just be bad. And when they come to second grade they always blame stuff on me. Like yesterday I got blamed, because some girl hit somebody and they were jumping her and thought it was me, me and my friends. Me and my cousin, and my friends we— they always blame stuff on us. And that—and that's not right. And I tell my mom and my mom don't do nothing. She just said "Be good."

We can note parenthetically that Latasha is a prototypical speaker of AAVE. She uses habitual BE in "I just be bad" along with the standard be of used to be which carries the same meaning.

Latasha is confronted with a contradiction that affects many people in our school system. Parents, friends, relatives, society, films, all deliver the message, "To be a successful human being, you must defend yourself; stand up for your rights." Parents say, "If someone hits you, you better hit them back, or you'll hear from me." Yet the schools, for very good reason, say the reverse. No one can deny the need to control violence in our schools, yet many say that the zero tolerance policy has created a pipeline to prison that feeds into mass incarceration.

Why does Latasha fight so much? Her response to the question,

"Did you ever get into a fight with a kid bigger than you?" tells us something about the deeper reasons.

> Well my brother's dead right? And my brother used to smoke cigarettes and, it was some little girl she a fake Muslim. She say, "That's why your brother dead cuz [sucks teeth] he was smoking cigarettes on the corner and stuff having—um—guns and stuff." And my brother do NOT have guns. All the people they say my brother was a peacemaker. They kept on talking about my brother and [sucks teeth] I—I just gotta fight with 'em.

Here too we can hardly escape noticing the consistent features of AAVE that mark Latasha as a speaker of this dialect. We note the absence of verbal /s/ and the typical variation of the copula, two zeroes to one contracted form. But these details may distract us from what she is telling us. Latasha reflects on the nature of the world she is living in. It is not only her brother who was shot dead last year, but her cousin as well.

> That's why I wanna be in some other world—not other world, but I wanna be in some o—some other country cuz around my way [sucks teeth] it's—it's drama around my way . . . I'm not a scared of 'em but I just want to move . . . Like my brother and my cousin dead and they kept on talking about them [sucks teeth] so I gotta fight with 'em.

Latasha was seven years old. She wore a necklace with pictures of her brother and her cousin, whose memory she defends. Latasha obeys a deep human imperative—to keep faith with the dead. How can she be persuaded to abandon that path and follow the school's inflexible rule: report every aggression to the teacher and never raise a hand in anger?

I don't have an answer to this question, but it is omnipresent in our efforts to give children confidence in an educational system that has, so far, abandoned them to isolation and despair. The stories that I write are designed to resonate with Latasha's view of the world, though they do not reach to the grim reality of her everyday life. As part of the road to literacy, these graphic novels are designed first to help unlock the secrets of the alphabet. But they are particularly aimed at the alienated and discouraged reader who suffers most from the deep divisions in our society. They tell the struggling reader, "Yes, life is unfair. But you can handle it. And you don't have to become a different person to do it. You can be yourself and learn to read."

I have tried to show that the growing differences between black and white in the inner cities of our society have created conditions favoring great linguistic diversity. I hope to have shown also that African American Vernacular English is not itself the cause of the educational problem. It is a faithful reflection of the deep divisions in our society. It is also the eloquent and versatile tool that speakers of the language use to give voice to their view of reality. By listening to that voice we can construct educational programs that bridge the gap between black and white, and lay the foundation of upward mobility that is the only solution for Latasha's despair.

6 ↔ LANGUAGE CHANGE AS LOCAL POLITICS

Chapters 3 and 4 displayed a widespread and surprising tendency toward divergence and differentiation in the English spoken on the continent of North America. This was surprising for two reasons. First, because the opposite direction of change—convergence—is commonly expected to follow from the unifying effect of the national media. That effect cannot be lightly dismissed. No matter what the effect of regional radio, national radio and television networks disseminate a more or less convergent broadcast pronunciation. The divergence of our regional dialects described in chapter 4 indicates that this broadcast standard has really very little influence on our actual language behavior. Chapter 5 did describe a convergent national pattern in the grammar of AAVE. Could this reflect an influence of the broadcast media? Probably not. Though some forms of African American English are widely heard in black situation comedies, these TV productions rarely display the new elements of AAVE that were cited in chapter 4. Dialect divergence is surprising for a second reason. It runs counter to the primary function of language as it has developed in the human species: the capacity to communicate information about states of affairs across distant times and places. We are not better off because we do not understand one another.

The puzzle of diverging languages returns us to the central questions concerning language change. The world is full of languages that were once mutually intelligible dialects of the same language but now take many years of study if their speakers are to understand one another. Hindi, Russian, Albanian, Irish, French, English, and Norwegian were once such dialects of Indo-European. Some of this differentiation is the result of long-term geographic separation. But as we have seen, divergence is also found among people who are in close contact with one another. It seems that some dialects do not just drift apart, but are pushed apart.

Once people have accepted the basic finding that dialects are becoming more different from each other, they demand an explanation: why is this happening? It is the search for an answer to that question that drives our research from the outset. The end of chapter 1 cited the scholars who have been trying to find that answer ever since the science of linguistics was developed. The traditional explanation of sound change was that it was the result of defects in human nature: laziness, ignorance, and stupidity. That point of view was challenged by sociolinguistic studies of language change in New York City and Philadelphia. Those studies changed the question from, Why is language changing? to Who is changing it? The leaders of linguistic change in those cities were not lower class, disreputable people, but were from the highest status local people: bank tellers, teachers, block captains. They were among the most active members of society, distinguished by their social involvement and their upward mobility rather than laziness or ignorance. The question as to why these community leaders were leading language change then became more urgent.

Part of the answer turned out to be mechanical. Chapter 2 presented a view of the Northern Cities Shift as a chain linking five elements together. A language—or the vowel system of a language—is an intricate piece of clockwork, whose parts are all interconnected. A change in one part of the mechanism leads to a change in another part, and over the centuries, linguistic change can be seen as a series of actions and reactions as change spreads through the system. Thus the Northern Cities Shift that we encountered in figure 5 was seen as a chain in which each step in the change was considered the cause of the one that followed.

Such structural accounts are important and convincing, and no account of language change that ignores them can hope to succeed. They show us language not as a list of isolated items, like new words in a dictionary, but as elements that are locked together in a set of mutual relations where change in one involves change in others. But since such structural explanations deal with features that are common to all languages, they do not have much to say about the *actuation* problem: why here, and now? and not there, and not then? (Weinreich, Labov, and Herzog 1968). A gap in the pattern of vowels may induce a change that will fill it, but this does not always happen. Crowding in one area of the vowel space leads to changes that relieve the crowding, but this does not always happen.

There are two basic strategies for going beyond generalities about what can happen to accounts of what did happen. Both of these strategies involve social and political factors. First, we need to search for the conditions that initiated the causal sequence in the first place (see Labov 2008; Labov 2010, chap. 5). Second, we need to identify the driving forces that keep the change moving across generations. In most cases, the social development of a language change is opportunistic: there is no inherent connection between the linguistic feature and the social value that is assigned to it. A generally accepted idea is that a chance variation in local patterns becomes associated with the social values of the group in which it originates, and then spreads to others who look to that group as a reference group (Sturtevant 1947). But before 1961 no one had observed this process actually happening.

This was the focus of the first study that I did on the social motivation of a sound change on Martha's Vineyard (Labov 1963). I noticed a particular way of speaking that had not been reported before on that island. It is not easy to describe in print without phonetic notation, but it may be heard in the online publication of the American Council of Learned Societies, where both the phonetic key and the speakers are attached to the printed text (Labov 2009). This speech pattern may best be described as a close-mouthed style of articulation. In most dialects, the vowels of *right* and *out* begin with a low vowel, the sound of "ah." What I was hearing was a pronunciation that began with the mouth half-closed, the "shwa" as in the first vowel of *about*. It was particularly interesting because the *Linguistic Atlas of New England,* a generation before, had reported a very different pronunciation for Vineyarders, and the change was actually reversing the direction of history. We can refer to the sound change in question as "centralization."[1]

I traced the degree and frequency of centralization by recording people in many parts of the island. One of the first people I talked to was Donald Poole, an eighth-generation descendant of Yankee whalers and fishermen. He was one of the key figures of the little fishing town of Menemsha; in fact, I was told that long-term summer people counted themselves as having arrived if Donald Poole said hello to them on the dock.[2]

> You see you people who come down here to Martha's Vineyard don't understand the background of the old families on the island. Our interests run that way, our thoughts still run that way, I'm speaking now of the descendants of the old families. Now what we're interested in, the rest of America, this part over here across the water that belongs to you and we don't have anything to do with, has forgotten all about the maritime tradition and the fact that if it hadn't been for the interest that the early settlers of this country took in the ocean, as whalemen, fisherman, and as seamen and merchant sailors, this country couldn't have existed, the Plymouth Colony would've been a failure.

To understand where this sound change was coming from and where it was going, I created an index of centralization based on impressionistic phonetics but confirmed by a sample of acoustic measures. The progress of the sound change on the island seemed variable in the extreme, correlated not only with age but also with gender, occupation, neighborhood, and ethnicity. My interviewing methods shifted accordingly to a broad range of social issues. In interviews with fishermen, farmers, local businessmen, across three generations; with Yankees, Gay Head Indians, and Portuguese, I found a connection between the sound change and the major concerns that troubled people in everyday life. The local people were under great pressure from the wealthy summer people from the mainland, who were buying up as much of the shoreline property as they could. Some younger people left the island to earn a living on the mainland, but others stayed and resisted this outside pressure. Centralization was strongest among those who stayed. Donald Poole was archetypical for his generation. His son, Everett Poole, was even more so. He had returned from college to set up a business selling fish on the Menemsha docks, and his centralization values were the most extreme.

Reviewing the interviews as a whole, I could see that some people expressed positive orientation to the island, determined to remain and work there; others were neutral; and a small number were negative, indicating a strong motivation to leave the island. The clearest correlation found between centralization and social factors is shown as table 3, which associates centralization with orientation toward Martha's Vineyard. Forty people with positive orientation had values of 62 and 63; 19 with a neutral position had values of 32 and 42; and 6 who were negative toward the island had centralization values of only 9 and 8.

Thus centralization emerged as a symbol of local identity, driven by an unconscious mechanism of *incrementation,* as the struggle to maintain local rights and privileges intensified across generations. This finding (Labov 1963) has been generally accepted, frequently cited, and taken as paradigmatic for the social motivation of sound change. Studies of other small communities under outside pressure have found a similar resurgence of linguistic markers of social identity.[3] Two fieldworkers have revisited Martha's Vineyard to see what has happened in recent years. One found that the phenomenon was no longer present (Blake and Josey 2003). The other found that it was—that it had continued vigorously for some time—but showed signs of recession among the youngest speakers (Pope, Meyerhoff, and Ladd 2007).

There can be little doubt that the use of language to symbolize local identity is a powerful force in the forging of linguistic diversity. It was not one of the factors that was foregrounded in the discussions

Table 3 Mean centralization values by orientation toward Martha's Vineyard

	Orientation to the island		
	Positive	Neutral	Negative
(ay) *right, side, island,* etc.	63	32	09
(aw) *out, south, loud,* etc.	62	42	08

of the causes of change in the 19th century. One reason may be that professors in leading universities have little investment in the local community: their rights and privileges are determined by their status on the national and international scene. It is only when linguists began to enter the local community and record the use of language in everyday life that the importance of local rights and privileges became clear. We see the importance of local identity in publicly aired issues involving hunting and fishing rights, variances for house renovations, rights to conduct business, election to local committees. Below the surface there may be an even wider range of attitudes and decisions for which recognition of local status is crucial.

Local Identity in Philadelphia?

The concept of local identity has the attractive feature of linking language change with communicative signals among nonhuman animals. Some such signals are interpreted as claims to occupy a territory and as warnings to others to stay away (Stokes 1974). Given such a notion of local identity, the question then remains as to how a local linguistic feature spreads throughout a large speech community like New York City or Philadelphia. Local identity can be broadened to the larger concept of *reference group* (Merton 1957). It has been argued that groups of speakers adopt the way of speaking of another group as a way of claiming membership in that group. We might take this view of the Philadelphia development of the vowel /aw/ in *out, doubt, south, down,* etc., discussed as an example of black/white differentiation in chapter 4. In the Philadelphia white dialect, this vowel has undergone a steady series of changes leading to the most advanced form, which can be exemplified by a pronunciation of the word *down* as the sound of "day" followed rapidly by the sound of "awn."

This advanced "day-awn" vowel is not a common feature of American English. It can be heard in some areas of the South, but not with the consistency or force with which it is enunciated in Philadelphia. It is in effect a local feature of the Philadelphia dialect. Let us then see how local it is within Philadelphia: where are the groups located who make use of this feature of local identity?

An instrumental measure of the progress of this sound change is seen in figure 25. The vertical axis is the expected value of the "second formant," an acoustic measure that corresponds roughly to front and back tongue position. If the beginning of this /aw/ diphthong is similar to the vowel of the word CAT, the second formant (F2) will be in the range 1600 to 1800. If it is the vowel of DAY, as in the most advanced version, F2 will be in the 2100 range. Figure 25a correlates this measure with age groups: the younger the speaker, the more advanced the sound change. In figure 25b, the horizontal axis is not age but social class. In this long-term study of 10 Philadelphia neighborhoods, social class was determined by a combined index of occupation, education, and house value (Labov 2001, chap. 5). Figure 25b displays a curvilinear pattern: the leaders of linguistic change are found in the middle and upper working classes. This confirmed the major hypothesis of the study: that linguistic change is not initiated in the highest or lowest strata of society but in centrally located groups—the highest status speakers of the local community.

Now we would like to know, how many Philadelphians are affected by this sound change? Are they all moving in the same direction, or is it only the leading groups who are doing this? To put it another way, is the sound change affecting *south, out,* and *down* a local phenomenon within Philadelphia, or is it a property of the city as a whole? Figure 26 answers these questions with a scattergram displaying the mean value of F2 for each of the 112 individuals in the Philadelphia Neighborhood Study by age, using different symbols for five different social class groups. The straight lines show the trend separately for each social class. All five lines slope upward to the left, indicating that for each social class, younger people use more advanced forms of the change. The solid black line represents the upper working class, with a slightly steeper slope than others, emerging to take the lead among younger speakers. We see that all groups are moving in the same direction. What is most striking is the dot-dashed line at the bottom, representing the upper class: it is parallel to the lines for the working-class groups.

The locality that is being identified here is not any particular neighborhood—Kensington, South Philadelphia, or Two Street—but the metropolis of Philadelphia as a whole. We might argue that the change started in one neighborhood—most likely the oldest settled Irish neighborhood of Kensington—and then spread to other areas

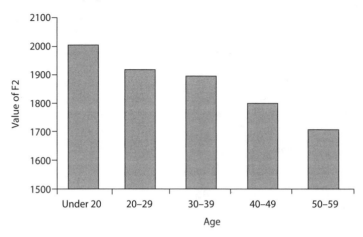

(a) Distribution by age

(b) Distribution by socioeconomic class

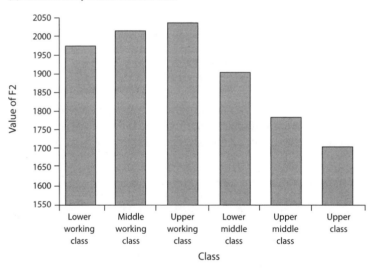

FIGURE 25. Fronting of the vowel of *out, south, down,* etc., in the Philadelphia Neighborhood Study ($N = 112$).

Vertical axis shows expected values of the second formant for each age range, calculated by adding age of regression coefficients to the constant.

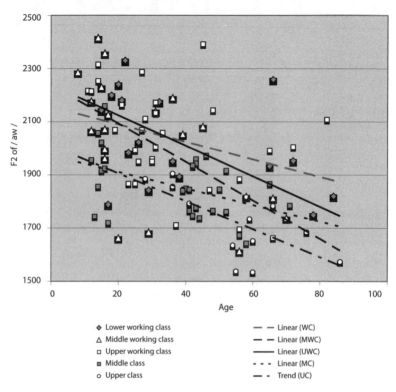

FIGURE 26. Scattergram of the fronting of the vowel of *out, south, down,* etc., as measured by second formant, by age and social class in the Philadelphia Neighborhood Study (*N* = 112), with partial regression lines for social class.

because of the tendency to take the Kensington dialect as a model. But though we might argue that this was the case for a spread to lower-middle-class speakers, it is not believable that such a mechanism operates for the upper middle class or upper class.[4] It would be absurd to explain the parallel movement of the upper class to an unconscious desire to sound like middle-class or working-class Philadelphians. The upper class is defined here as people with more money than they can count, who send their children to elite private schools and who tell their children that they are *not* middle class. Something else is driving this change across the whole metropolitan community, and so far, we have to admit that we don't know what it is.

This uniform direction of change is not a peculiarity of one particular sound change. It is also found in the tendency of younger

Philadelphians to raise the vowel of *lane, fade,* and *slave* toward *lean, feed,* and *sleeve.* This is again a local feature of the Philadelphia dialect. It involves a change limited to syllables ending with a consonant. It does not apply to words with no final consonant, like *play, OK, say.*[5]

The uniformity of linguistic patterning in Philadelphia was confirmed in the 1970s by a random sample of 60 telephone users (Labov 2001, chap. 5) and since then reinforced by other studies of a representative sample of that community (Conn 2005). The geographic coherence of Philadelphia does not appear to be an isolated phenomenon. It seems to be characteristic of every great metropolis: London, Paris, Berlin, New York. This is in spite of the well-known claim of Henry Higgins (modeled on the linguists Henry Sweet and Daniel Jones) that he could locate any London speaker within a block. The common conviction that big cities have local dialects appears to stem from the use of geographic labels for social-class dialects. Thus "Brooklynese" is a common term for working-class New York City speech, which has been found to be much the same in Jersey City, Queens, Staten Island, and the Lower East Side (Labov 1966; *Atlas,* chap. 17).

If Not Local, Then What?

Our search for the driving forces in linguistic change therefore cannot rest with the idea that change is motivated by a need for emblems of local identity. The social forces that lead to metropolitan uniformity cannot easily be assigned to local machinery; the citywide uniformity that we find implies an underlying political process. It has been pointed out to me that linguistic variables cannot carry very much weight among family members or other intimate groups. Members already know so much about each other that the use of a given linguistic form does not add very much to their evaluation of each other. But when members of a community encounter people that they do not see every day, at block parties, neighborhood rallies, or political meetings, their forms of speech may become more informative. In the past five decades, sociolinguists have studied the exchange of linguistic tokens in many local social networks, but not in that broader web of social relations that crosses and binds the city as a whole.

The politics of language change can be illuminated by the language of politicians. It has been observed many times that political leaders weave a tapestry of linguistic variation, using features of their local origins to express solidarity with their constituents, balanced with enough recognition of the national standard to establish themselves as educated and capable executives. But this sense of "local" is no longer the sense that was encountered among the 200 inhabitants of the village of Menemsha on Martha's Vineyard, who knew each other's smallest habits from childhood. Big city mayors and members of congress can be local only in some extended, symbolic sense for the general population.

If we now turn to the larger uniformities of regional linguistic change, the role of local identity becomes even more problematic. The next chapter will examine the political factors involved in the most extreme example of divergence in North American English as described in chapter 3—the Northern Cities Shift.

Chapter 2 looked at the general consensus on sociolinguistic variables like (ING), which showed a surprising uniformity in use and recognition. Chapter 3 then opened the door to the even more surprising findings on the growth of regional diversity in North American dialects. The most striking case was the Northern Cities Shift, remarkable from several points of view: the number of sound categories involved, the extent of their rotation, and the intricate relations among them. This chapter will attempt to account for other surprising aspects of the NCS: the vast territory that it covers, the uniformity within that territory, and the sharp boundary that divides it from other dialect patterns.

The Northern Cities Shift as a Marker of Local Identity

The Northern Cities Shift was discovered by a number of exploratory studies in the 1970s. None of them dealt with the social context that might be driving this chain shift. However, in the early 1980s Penelope Eckert carried out a long-term ethnographic study of "Belten High School" in a Detroit suburb, focusing on the NCS as a main linguistic variable in the speech of these students. In the course of her study, Eckert discovered the latest link in the chain: the backing of *lunch* to sound like *launch, bus* to sound like *boss, bunk* to sound like *bonk.* Eckert's study showed that elements of the NCS are sensitive to the give and take of local social relations and can serve as symbols of local identity. In 1989 she published *Jocks and Burnouts: Social Categories and Identities in the High School,* widely used in schools of education today for its general analysis of the social structure of the high school. The book identified two polar groups of students in Belten High. *Jocks* seek success and social recognition by conforming to the institutional norms established by adults, in school government, varsity athletics, and performing arts. *Burnouts* pursue rewards and recognition in their own social networks by following the reverse pattern, escaping from and avoiding those institutional norms as far as they can. The majority of students are *In-Betweens*, who define themselves by the degree that they share values and behaviors with one of the two polar groups. Jocks and Burnouts show radically different patterns in regard to clothing, smoking, territories occupied, and patterns of cruising the local areas.

Figure 27 lays out Eckert's overall findings on the social distribution of the NCS (Eckert 2000). The five elements of the NCS are placed along the horizontal axis in the order in which they seem to have occurred: the shift of short-a in *bat* toward the vowel of *yeah*, the shift of short-o in *got* toward *bat*, the shift of long open-o in *bought* toward *got*, the shift of short-e in *bet* toward *but*, and the shift of short-u in *but* toward *bought*. The vertical axis is the percentage of advanced tokens by phonetic judgment of the analysts.

One can see that for the most recent elements in the series, the backing of short-e and short-u, Burnouts are well ahead of Jocks, and this proved to be significant in Eckert's analyses. But for the older, earlier elements of the sound change, the difference is a matter of gender: girls are well ahead of boys, with no significant difference between the two social classes, Jocks and Burnouts.

These quantitative patterns are linked to observed variation in everyday behavior. Eckert shows that girls who are most extreme in their Burnout behavior—the "Burned out Burnouts"—are also most extreme in the backing of short-u. The concept advanced by Eckert is that the advanced forms of sound change carry social meaning, symbolic claims of the speakers' status as members, exemplary members or archetypical members of a particular group, parallel with their conformity to the group norms for clothing, smoking, drinking, doing drugs, dating and cruising. Thus the driving force behind the sound changes is seen to lie in the dynamics of local social networks. More specifically, sound changes are seen to originate specifically as fea-

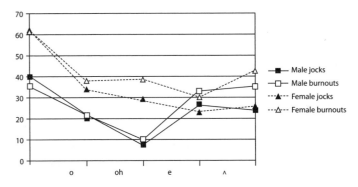

FIGURE 27. Percentage of advanced tokens for five stages of the Northern Cities Shift in a Detroit high school by group membership and gender (based on Eckert 2000).

tures of local identification of the nonconformist group, and then spread to other portions of the social network who take the Burnouts as a reference group, particularly the In-Betweens who are least distant from the Burnouts.

Nonlocal Aspects of the Northern Cities Shift

We now have to confront a recurring problem for local explanations. Figure 26 in the last chapter showed that the sound changes found in local neighborhoods—Kensington, Overbrook, South Philadelphia, Pennsport, and Chestnut Hill—are actually characteristic of the metropolis as a whole, the speech pattern of 1.5 million people. The fundamental differences are those of social class, not neighborhood. Figure 8 of chapter 3 showed that the Northern Cities Shift was general over the vast area of the Inland North. Figure 9 of chapter 3 showed also that the change in progress was leading to increasing divergence of vowel systems across the North/Midland line.

Figure 8 shows in addition a black and white barred "lexical" boundary. This is the general vocabulary boundary drawn from the *Dictionary of American Regional English* (Carver 1987). It has nothing to do with the NCS, but represents the oppositions of Northern *stone fence* to Midland *rock fence*, Northern *potluck* vs. Midland *carry in*, Northern *belly flop* vs. Midland *belly buster* (for a face-down sled ride), Northern *darning needle* vs. Midland *snake feeder* (dragon fly), Northern *co-day!* vs. Midland *sheepie!* (call to sheep), and a dozen others. These are traditional agricultural and rural terms that date back to the original settlement of these areas in the mid-19th century, a hundred years before the NCS was first observed.

It is evident that no local mechanism can be driving the Northern Cities Shift in the same direction with the same results over this vast area. If there is a social motivation that is involved in this long-term and widespread process, it cannot depend on face-to-face contact between the speakers involved. Rather we are looking for a historical process that affects 34 million people throughout their life histories. By a parallel logic, the coincidence of the lexical boundaries and the modern sound changes points back to history for an explanation. When did the Northern Cities Shift begin and where did it come from?

The Origin and History of the Northern Cities Shift

Our most likely guess is that the conditions for the Northern Cities Shift originated at the time of the building of the Erie Canal, from 1817 to 1825. The Erie Canal was planned and proposed as the major route for westward expansion by DeWitt Clinton, governor of New York. The plan took advantage of the fact that the Hudson River was ice-free year long, being a saltwater estuary, while Philadelphia, on the Delaware River, was icebound for a good part of the year. From the time that the canal was completed, New York City passed Philadelphia in size and importance, and has maintained its advantage ever since. The major cities in New York State that are centers of the Northern Cities Shift—Utica, Rochester, Syracuse, and Buffalo—are all located on the route of the Erie Canal.

The consequences for urban growth in New York State were correspondingly great. At the end of the War of 1812 Rochester had a population of 331, largely of New England origin. The construction of the canal required large numbers of laborers, and many immigrants of Irish background arrived, forming the section of Rochester called Dublin. From 1820 to 1830 the population grew from 1,507 to 9,207 (McKelvey 1949a). Today nearly 80% of upstate New York's population is still to be found within 25 miles of the Erie Canal. This spectacular expansion was small compared to the growth of population in surrounding Monroe County and in the seven neighboring counties from 1810 to 1830, reaching a peak in 1850. This tenfold increase in population is crucial. Normally, the first group arriving in an area sets the cultural pattern for all those who come later (the principle of First Effective Settlement, Zelinsky 1992). But a tenfold increase allows earlier patterns to be overridden.

The general hypothesis to be put forward here (and further developed in Labov 2008, 2010a) is that the triggering event of the Northern Cities Shift was the population mixture in New York State brought about by the construction of the Erie Canal. Many different systems for the pronunciation of words spelled with short-a were found among the newcomers. These dialects differed as to which words are pronounced with the vowel of *cat* and which with a higher, longer vowel similar to the vowel of *yeah* or *idea*. We will call this higher, longer vowel the *tense* form, as opposed to the *lax* vowel in *cat*.

(1) *The nasal system* from northeastern New England and Providence. Here all short-a words before nasal consonants /m/ and /n/ are tense, while all other words with short-a are lax. In extreme nasal systems, the girl's name *Ann* is pronounced in exactly the same way as the boy's name *Ian*.

(2) *The broad-a system* from Boston and the surrounding area. Here we have in addition to the nasal system a number of "broad-a" words inherited from southeastern British speech: *half, can't, aunt, laugh*, and many others can have the vowel of *father*, rather than the vowel of *cat*.

(3) *The continuous system* from southwestern New England. Many communities show a continuous range of raising short-a from lax to tense without the sharp break characteristic of the nasal system.

(4) *The split system* in New York City. This is a complex division into tense and lax sets. Tense vowels are heard in *cab, bad, bag, pass, laugh, [tin] can, plan, planning*, and other words ending with these consonants, but lax vowels are heard in *cap, cat, pack, thank, [I] can*, and *planet*.

The mixture of linguistic systems led to the formation of a fifth system adapted by all children learning the language. This common dialect, or koine, formed a fifth, and simplest, short-a system:

(5) *The general raising system.* All words with short-a are tense—*pat, pad, man, that, smack, challenge, attitude, actually,* etc.—and none are lax.

This, we hypothesize, was the uniform system throughout upper and western New York State, as it is found there today. Now let us consider how this system moved out of New York State to occupy the entire Great Lakes region. The economic impetus to westward movement was powerful. Before the canal, the cost to ship one ton of goods from Buffalo to New York City was $100; using the canal, the same amount could be shipped for $10 (McKelvey 1949b). The great drop in cost of transportation prompted westward migration and the development of farmland throughout the Inland North.

Figure 28 is a map created by the cultural geographers Kniffen and Glassie (1966), tracing three streams of westward migration. The map is based on observed differences in techniques of house and log cabin construction. The stream of settlement from New England populated the Northern dialect region. The Midland was settled by two overlapping streams: one from the Quaker hearth of Pennsylvania, the other, Upland Southerners from Appalachia. The boundary between them follows the North/Midland dialect boundary. It runs across the northern tier of counties in Pennsylvania, slides below the Western Reserve in Ohio, shifts north in Indiana above the "Hoosier apex," and descends to include the upper third of Illinois in the North.

In attempting to account for the linguistic uniformity of the North, we have to take into account the size of the unit that migrated. The Yankee migration westward moved populations as large as 20,000 as a whole.

Entire communities of young New Englanders . . . emigrated to the area of New York west of the Adirondack and Catskill mountains. (Carnes and Garrity 1996, 90)

Mass migrations were indeed congenial to the Puritan tradition. Whole parishes, parson and all, had sometimes migrated from Old England. Lois Kimball Mathews mentioned 22 colonies in Illinois alone, all of which originated in New England or in New York, most of them planted between 1830 and 1840. (Power 1953, 14)

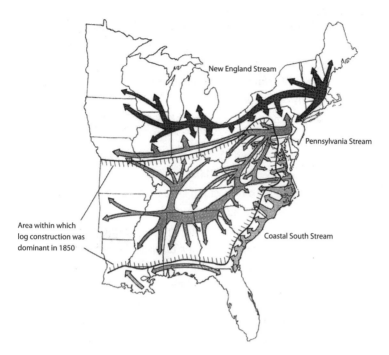

New England Stream

Pennsylvania Stream

Area within which
log construction was
dominant in 1850

Coastal South Stream

FIGURE 28. Patterns of westward settlement, as reflected in house construction
(from Kniffen and Glassie 1966, fig. 27).

Those migrating to the Midland moved in much smaller units.

> The Upland Southerners left behind a loose social structure of rural
> "neighborhoods" based on kinship; when Upland Southerners
> migrated—as individuals or in individual families—the neighborhood
> was left behind. (Frazer 1993, 63)

David Hackett Fischer's study of four cultural streams of American settlement (1989) places considerable emphasis on the size of the
groups that moved, and the permanence of the residential outcome.
He shows that the Yankees moved in whole towns, and built perma-
nent settlements with houses by the roadsides. This created the en-
vironment in which generation after generation of child language
learners transmitted the system intact, steadily incrementing the
changes in a constant direction. On the other hand, Upland Southerners moved in isolated clusters, and often relocated with houses
scattered along creeks and springs. As a consequence, Midland cit-

ies show a wide variety of dialect formation: Philadelphia, Pittsburgh, Columbus, Cincinnati, Indianapolis, and St. Louis are all quite different from one another.[1]

This does not of course tell us what forces were pushing the linguistic change in opposite directions in the North and the Midland. We can get some sense of those forces through descriptions of communities in which the two groups of settlers, Yankees and Southerners, were in contact. Midland historians describe a marked opposition of cultural style between the Midland and the North. Here I draw on the work of two writers in particular. One is Richard Lyle Power, who published a study of Indiana communities under the title *Planting Corn Belt Culture: The Impress of the Upland Southerner and Yankee in the Old Northwest* (1953). The other is Thomas Morain, author of a 1988 work entitled *Prairie Grass Roots: An Iowa Small Town in the Early Twentieth Century*. Like most historians and everyday observers, Power and Morain label this cultural opposition as one between "Northerners" or "Yankees" on the one hand, and "Southerners" on the other. It appears that the Upland South contribution to the Midland culture was more distinctive and salient than the Quaker Pennsylvanian elements. These Midland historians are not slow to express their point of view on Yankee cultural patterns, in terms that can hardly be described as neutral. They are particularly harsh on the Yankee tendency to impose their own views of morality on the rest of the community.

> . . . among the new arrivals to Jefferson [County, IN] was a species of settler strikingly different in outlook from small southern [upland] farmers . . . these newcomers not only displayed a disgusting predilection for self-improvement schemes but were also fond of pointing out their virtues to those who took life at a less feverish pace. . . .
>
> Taxed with being busybodies and meddlers, apologists own that the instinct for meddling, as divine as that of self-reservation, runs in the Yankee blood; that the typical New Englander was entirely unable, when there were wrongs to be corrected, to mind his own business. (Power 1953, 6)

Yankee historians also testify to this strong tendency to superimpose Yankee ideology on the rest of the world.

Along with their crackers, their codfish, and their theology, they carried their peculiar ideas of government and managed, in spite of Kentucky statutes in Illinois, to impose their township system throughout the state . . . [T]hey did the same to or for Michigan, and also established the whipping post, in words taken from Vermont's original laws. (Holbrook 1950, 16)

On the other hand, the Yankee view of the Midland was equally critical. In Le Baron's *History of McLean County, Illinois* (1879), we read:

The Northerner thought of the Southerner as a lean, lank, lazy creature, burrowing in a hut, and rioting in whiskey, dirt and ignorance. (97)

The first thing that Yankee settlers did in founding a city was to build schools, colleges, and universities. It's interesting to see how language was involved in this cultural opposition.

At Greensburg in southeastern Indiana, the Reverend J. R. Wheelock advised his eastern sponsors that his wife had opened a school of 20 or 30 scholars in which she would use "the most approved N.E. school books," to be obtained by a local merchant from Philadelphia. "She makes defining a distinct branch of study and this gives her a very favorable oppy. of correcting the children & thro' them, the parents of 'a heap' of Kentuckyisms." (Power 1953, 114)

In Morain's (1988) summary of Yankee practices, one can see a close resemblance between Yankee implementation of morality and the cultural style of the Christian Far Right today.

Imbued with the notion that theirs was a superior vision, Yankees dutifully accepted their responsibility for the moral and intellectual life of the nation, . . . with or without an invitation from the uneducated, the undisciplined, the disinterested, or the unmotivated.

Cultural uplift Yankee style also meant attacking sin and sloth. The initial settlement of Iowa coincided with three very active decades for American reform movements. Health fads, prison reform, women's rights, crusades for new standards of dress—the northern states teemed with advocates of one cause or another. (256)

The Place of Slavery in Yankee Ideology

When we read that Northern communities "teemed" with "fads," we recognize a heavily loaded vocabulary that signals an emotional distance from Yankee concerns. But we also read, finally,

> Most important among the reform movements of the day were the issues of abolition and temperance. (Morain 1988, 256)

In spite of the skepticism of Midland historians, there emerges something remarkably solid in this cultural opposition. The campaign for the abolition of slavery was not a fad; it was a matter of life and death for many people, white and black. There was an intimate connection between these social causes and the powerful evangelical movement called the Second Great Awakening. Western New York State in particular was known as the "Burned-Over District" in recognition of the religious fervor that prevailed there.

> Entire communities of young New Englanders . . . emigrated to the area of New York west of the Adirondack and Catskill mountains [arriving] in western New York, often by means of the Erie Canal. . . . The restless settlers of the "Burned-Over District" readily sought release in millennial and communitarian religion. (Carnes and Garrity 1996, 90)

Slavery was the central issue.

> In February 1841, [an interdenominational convention] adopted a totally ultra-ist position, condemning the *Baptist Register* and all others who acknowledged evil without taking action, and concluded that "the abolition cause . . . must prevail before the halcyon day of millennial glory can dawn upon the world." (ibid.)

We also read in Cross's (1950) work on the Burned-Over District:

> No other section of the country would throughout the years before the Civil War prove to be so thoroughly and constantly sensitive to antislavery agitation. As the major issue of the century, furthermore, this crusade attracted more attention than others. (224–25)

The Intersection of Religion and Politics

The religious revivals of the first half of the 19th century flowed seamlessly into politics in the second half. An early account of this intersection is found in the work of Richard Jensen, *The Winning of the Midwest* (1971), a history of social and political conflict in Indiana two decades after the end of the Civil War. Jensen sees religion as the fundamental source of political conflict in the Midwest. "The most revolutionary change in nineteenth century America was the conversion of the nation from a largely dechristianized land in 1789 to a stronghold of Protestantism by mid-century" (62). An important opposition was between "pietists" and "liturgicals," as it was expressed in struggles within many different denominations. Pietists were revivalists, emphasizing the experience of personal conversion and flatly rejecting ritualism. In contrast, "Liturgicals stressed the positive values of the institutionalized formalities of the old orthodoxies, whether Calvinist, Anglican, Lutheran, Catholic or Jewish" (64). They worked for Sunday blue laws, the abolition of saloons, and before the Civil War, a check to the growth of slavery, or indeed its abolition. Jensen sees a close connection between this religious polarity and the formation of the Republican/Democratic opposition.

> It seem reasonable to hypothesize that when party lines re-formed in the 1850s, the great majority of . . . pietists entered the Republican Party, while the great majority of liturgicals became Democrats. (69)

A more detailed view of how religious movements engaged with national politics is to be found in the work of Richard Carwardine, *Evangelicals and Politics in Antebellum America* (1993). Carwardine documents the tendency of many pietists to withdraw from politics but sees the larger evangelical movement—including Methodists, Baptists, and Presbyterians—driven toward political engagement (14–17).

> Most antebellum evangelicals . . . remained profoundly influenced by the Puritan conception of the state as a moral being and by its corollary, that Christians had a political duty to develop and maintain virtue and the highest standards in the conduct of civil affairs. (18)

The evangelical churches were of course split by section.

> . . . northern evangelicals . . . gravitated towards the Republican party,
> while those in the South encouraged and sanctioned what they regarded
> as the necessary defensive actions of politicians, Democrats in particular,
> in their own section. (35)

In turn, the Republican Party absorbed this orientation toward government as an agency for the public good.

> The emergence and ultimate success of the Republicans were dependent
> on a particular understanding of politics, one which evangelicals had
> played a major role in shaping. That political ethic was rooted in the . . .
> theology of the Second Great Awakening, marked by an optimistic post-
> millennialism and an urgent appeal to disinterested action. (320)

The Democratic Party also reached out to evangelicals, but primarily to those who took the individualist stance that we saw was prototypical of Midland settlement cultures.

> The Democrats' broad posture was designed to attract a different breed
> of evangelical, one for whom the state's only proper role was to protect
> men and women from religious tyranny. . . . Its anti-commercial stance
> also won sympathy from many of the same constituency: lower-class ru-
> ral folk, particularly but not exclusively in the rural South . . . who deeply
> resented the imperialism of the Yankee missionaries, their schemes for
> temperance, Sunday Schools and other reforms. (111–12)

Though both Republicans and Democrats declared themselves to be the representatives of the "common man," they were opposed in their view of the role of government in ways that are sharply reversed today. At that time, Whig Republicans were ready to use government power to develop national growth, and appealed to ordinary workers and farmers who would benefit from their policies, including protectionism. Democrats were then more fearful of government power and won the support of believers in laissez-faire and free trade.

In 1852 Harriet Beecher Stowe electrified the country with a fierce denunciation of slavery—at its best as well as its worst—in *Uncle Tom's Cabin*. Her "concluding remarks" were a clarion call for Northern opposition to slavery:

Farmers of Massachusetts, of New Hampshire, of Vermont, of Connecticut who read this book by the blaze of your winter evening fire—stronghearted generous sailors and ship-owners of Maine—is this a thing for you to countenance and encourage? Brave and generous men of New York, farmers of rich and joyous Ohio, and ye of the wide prairie states—answer, is this a thing for you to protect and countenance?

The last sentence of *Uncle Tom's Cabin* exemplifies the religious orientation of Republican rhetoric:

Not by combining together, to protect injustice and cruelty and making a common capital of sin, is this Union to be saved—but by repentance, justice and mercy, for, not surer is the eternal law by which the millstone sinks in the ocean, than that stronger law, by which injustice and cruelty shall bring on nations the wrath of Almighty God.

In the extreme polarization of the war, no distinction was made between Upland or backcountry South and the coastal South that was the center of the institution of slavery. Harriet Beecher Stowe's brother, the celebrated abolitionist preacher Henry Ward Beecher, proclaimed in 1863:

We are to have charge of this continent. The South has been proved, and has been found wanting. She is not worthy to bear rule. She has lost the scepter in our national government, she is to lose the scepter in the States themselves; and this continent is to be from this time forth governed by Northern men, with Northern ideas, and with a Northern gospel.

There are, however, many aspects of political and moral behavior in which the North of the Civil War did not behave as a unity. Here the North/Midland boundary aligns the Midland with the South, sharply opposed to the Yankee settlement region in a way that echoes the linguistic divisions of chapter 3.

The Inland North and the Death Penalty

In addition to the central questions of slavery and temperance, the opposition between the North and the Midland emerges in another ideological issue: the death penalty. In the long history of efforts to abolish and reinstall capital punishment, the area of Yankee settlement has generally opposed it, while other regions have heavily favored it.

Our current pursuit of ideological history is enhanced by the state-by-state account of death penalty abolition and restoration in table 4. The upper half of the table lists the main states that participate in the long history of abolition; the lower half those that have only been partially or occasionally involved. The first legislation to abolish the death penalty was passed in the middle of the 19th century in four northern states: Iowa, Wisconsin, Michigan, and Maine. It was followed by a wave of reinstallation, leaving only Wisconsin and Rhode Island with complete abolition. In 1887 Maine returned to its abolitionist position. Then in the last quarter of the 19th century, a new wave of abolition affected a number of states, but a new wave of restoration from 1916 to 1939 again left only northern states in the anti–death penalty camp. A third wave of abolition involved seven northern states and four others. Then in 1972 the Supreme Court decision *Furman v. Georgia* abolished the death penalty as cruel and unusual punishment in violation of the Eighth and Fourteenth Amendments. One by one, states modified their legislation to permit the reintroduction of the death penalty.

Figure 29 displays the situation in 2004. The figures show for each state the number of crimes for which the death penalty is legislated. The states in white without figures have resisted pressures to reinstitute the death penalty: a core of seven states in the Northern and New England dialect areas and three others, North Dakota, Kansas, and West Virginia. While New York State has retained the death penalty for two crimes, the largest part of its population (the metropolitan area) falls outside the dialect region we are considering.

The important point about this history is the continuity of the anti–death penalty ideology in the areas of Yankee settlement for the past two hundred years.

The Coincidence of Dialect Boundaries with Political Cultures

In 1966 Daniel Elazar published *American Federalism: A View from the States,* an analysis of the political cultures of North America (2nd ed., 1972). This work defined three basic cultural types:

Table 4 History of legislation abolishing the death penalty

		States																
		ME	RI	MI	WI	IA	MN	ND	SD	KS	NE	NM	TN	OR	WV	NY	VT	MA	NJ
1846–70	First wave of abolition	√		(√)	√	√													
1878–83	First wave of restoration		√	(√)	√														
1887	Restoration in Maine	√	√	(√)	√														
1897–1915	Second wave of abolition	√	√	(√)	√		√	(√)	√	√	√	√	√	√					
1916–39	Second wave of restoration	√	√	(√)	√		√	(√)	√	√	√	√							
1957–69	Third wave of abolition	√	√	(√)	√	√	√	(√)							√	√	(√)	(√)	
1972	Supreme Court decision							√							√	√	√	√	√
1973–2008	Recent restoration	√	√	√	√	√	√	√											

Note: √ = states with no death penalty; (√) = death penalty for treason only.

FIGURE 29. Status of the death penalty in 2004.

White states = no death penalty. Numbers = no. of crimes for which the death penalty is legislated. Solid lines = the North and New England regions.

MORALISTIC. This group expects the government to help people achieve good lives. Governmental service is "public service." The community can intervene in private affairs if this serves communal goals.

INDIVIDUALISTIC. This group views government in utilitarian and in-dividualist terms. Politics is a business like any other, which is dominated by "firms" (parties). Government should not interfere much in individuals' lives.

TRADITIONALISTIC. This group combines hierarchical views of society with ambivalence about "government-as-marketplace." Popular participation is scarcely important in comparison with elite participation. There is also a strong preference for maintaining the status quo, as evidenced by the South's general resistance to the civil rights movement.

The Moralistic and Individualistic categories are a close fit to the accounts of North and Midland attitudes and ideologies provided by Carwardine, Jensen, and other historians we have been reviewing. The characteristics of the Moralistic group fit closely the Yankee reliance on control of morality through governmental action, and the Individualistic group the opposition to such control attributed to Upland Southern inhabitants of the Midland.

Elazar also provides the data for figure 30, a map of the geographic distribution of these ideologies in North America. It can readily be seen that the distribution of the three political cultures coincides with the three dialect regions North, Midland, and South. The Moralistic/ Individualistic boundary in particular follows the path of the North/ Midland boundary. Elazar recognizes that this distribution follows from the patterns of westward settlement seen in our figure 28. He traces the northernmost pattern to New England Yankee culture in ways that are consistent with the concept of "cultural hearth" developed by D. H. Fischer (1989). He also shows how the various immigrant groups of the later 19th and early 20th centuries—German, Irish, Italian, Polish—adapted the cultural patterns of the earlier settlers, following the Doctrine of First Effective Settlement (Zelinsky 1992). What is particularly important for our current analysis is that the geographic pattern of figure 30 is based on a large series of case studies of political behavior which are entirely independent of the dialect data.

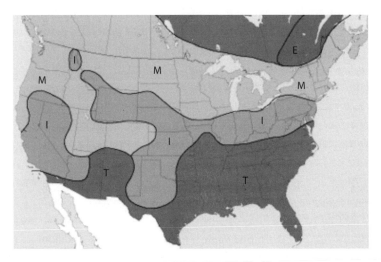

FIGURE 30. Distribution of political cultures in North America (from Kilpinen 2009, based on Elazar 1972, fig. 11).

M = moralistic. I = individualistic. T = traditional.

The Northern Cities Shift, the Blue States, and the Red States

At the beginning of the 21st century, we find another geographic coincidence of the Northern dialect area with political ideology: the relationship between the Blue States as defined by the presidential elections of 2004 and 2008 and the area in which the Northern Cities Shift predominates in North American English. The six states in the upper half of table 4—those who showed the most consistent opposition to the death penalty—are all Blue States, voting for the Democratic candidate in 2004 and 2008. Since dialect boundaries rarely follow state borders, the match between the Northern dialect region and the states voting Democratic is only a rough approximation of the dialect areas to political stance. A more accurate view of this relation can be obtained by considering the vote county by county. Here maps are not too useful, since the rural areas dominate the geographical scene, while the *Atlas* linguistic data is based on cities of population over 50,000. The analysis to follow will take as units the counties in which the cities studied by the *Atlas* are embedded. In many cases the city is coextensive with the county, but in all cases the city represents the largest part of the population and is most often the county seat.

Table 5 displays the distribution of Kerry or Bush county majorities in the 2004 election in three dialect regions: the Inland North, as defined by the Northern Cities Shift; the North generally, defined by the linguistic preconditions for the NCS; and the Midland. Midland counties are markedly different from North and Inland North, favoring Bush by 62% to 38%.

A more detailed view of the situation is given in figure 31, a scattergram of the 69 counties with *Atlas* subjects by linguistic region. The horizontal axis is the Bush/Kerry vote. The vertical axis is the log

Table 5 Democratic vs. Republican vote in presidential election of 2004, by counties surveyed in the *Atlas of North American English*

	Inland North	North	Midland
Kerry majority	20	15	8
Bush majority	6	7	13

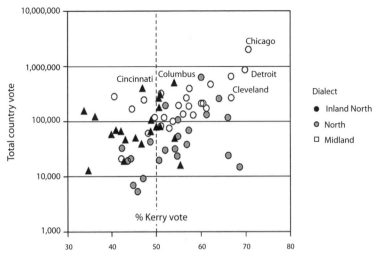

FIGURE 31. Percentage of county vote for Kerry by total county in the 2004 presidential election, for counties in the Inland North, North, and Midland dialect areas.

of the total county vote. We can observe a clear shift from lower left to upper right, indicating that the Kerry vote was favored by city size. We also note that the black circles—NCS counties—are well to the right of the empty squares (Midland counties), indicating that NCS cities favor Kerry. The relative positions of the largest cities—Chicago, Detroit, and Cleveland vs. Cincinnati and Columbus—are characteristic of the whole trend.

Table 6 shows the results of regression analyses of the data in figure 31. The Midland is the residual group against which North and Inland North are compared. Analysis 1 shows that use of an Inland North or Northern dialect (as against the Midland dialect) and city size are major contributors to the Kerry vote.

At the level of county-by-county voting patterns, dialect areas coincide more precisely with Democratic preference than we observed at the state level, and we can now be sure that this is not an accidental phenomenon. The table predicts that in cities of comparable size on either side of the North/Midland boundary, like Columbus and Cleveland, we can expect a mean difference of about 6% in Democratic voting—enough to affect the state outcome. The second analysis in this table indicates that if observers do *not* take city size into account,

Table 6 Regression analyses of percentage county vote for Kerry in 2004 presidential election by dialect groups

	Analysis 1		Analysis 2	
Variable	coeff.	prob.	coeff.	prob.
Log county total vote (millions)	3.7	≤ 0.0001		
North dialect	10.7	≤ 0.0001	8.0	.0001
Inland North dialect	6.1	0.0037	9.1	.0000

Note: Analysis 1 with total votes as independent variable, Analysis 2 without.

they will observe an even larger difference. The voting pattern of the Inland North is a joint product of its urban character and ideological background, but the fact that big cities favored the Democrats in 2004 is also the by-product of ideological history.

The political orientation represented by the Blue States/Red States geographic split was not notably different in the preceding election of 2000, but major shifts can be observed in the following presidential election of 2008. Figure 32 is a scattergram of North, Inland North, and Midland city counties, comparable to figure 31 but with the horizontal axis now representing the percentage of vote for Obama. The data are shifted strongly to the right; Columbus moves to the Obama column, and Chicago is up to 78% for Obama. The correlation with dialect and city size is much reduced, but one can still see the concentration of black Inland North symbols on the right, and Midland squares on the left.

The Democratic/Republican correlation of dialect regions with voting patterns may not reflect an association of language and ideology, but may be the result of independent historical trends. The dialect of the Inland North and the politics of the Inland North may have developed distinctive patterns with no direct relation between these two forms of behavior. If there is such an association of the Northern Cities Shift and ideology, it should be reflected in the Inland North, where people with Democratic orientation should show more advanced forms than those with Republican orientation. Table 7

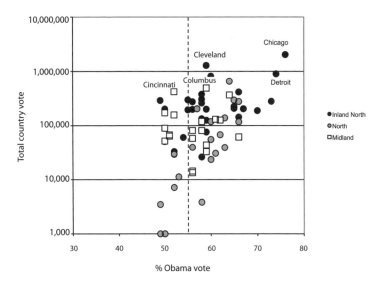

FIGURE 32. Percentage of county vote for Obama by total county vote in the 2008 presidential election, for counties in the Inland North, North, and Midland dialect areas.

provides an answer to this question in the output of a multiple regression analysis that begins with the mean value of each sound change as measured for a given speaker as the dependent variable, what we are trying to explain; enters into the analysis all the social factors that have proved to have significant effects for one feature or another; and then adds the ratio of Democratic votes to Republican votes for each county in which the speaker is located.

Table 7 is the output of a regression analysis for the Inland North alone. Three of the sound shifts of the Northern Cities Shift are considered: the raising of short-a, the backing of short-e, and the backing of short-u. Age effects are listed first. The first variable appears to have reached its maximum with no age effect, but for the other two there is a significant age factor: older speakers show higher values, and younger speakers lower (backer) ones, as originally indicated for the backing of short-u in figure 9. The negative values for female gender indicate that women favor the first two of these sound changes. Only one strong effect for occupation emerges, disfavoring the raising of short-a, and no effect emerges for education. The last factor is

Table 7 Regression coefficients for three features of the Northern Cities Shift for 62 speakers in the Inland North by social factors and ratio of Democratic to Republican vote in speaker's county

	Raising short-a	Backing short-e	Backing short-u
Constant	595	1555	1188
Age (*25 yrs.)	n.s.	68*	40*
Female	−45***	−77**	n.s.
Occupation	1.18***	n.s.	n.s.
Education	n.s.	n.s.	n.s.
Ratio Dem./Rep.	−33	−90*	n.s.

no star = $p < .10$; *$p < .05$; **$p < .01$; ***$p < .001$; n.s. (not significant) = $p > .10$

the ratio of Democratic to Republican votes in the county in which the speaker resides. This weakly favors the raising of short-a and significantly favors the backing of short-e. It does not reach significance for the backing of short-u. But combining the three variables, there is a significant favoring of the sound shifts in counties with a high proportion of Democratic to Republican votes. We conclude that the correlation of language and political ideology is not limited to a comparison of the North and the Midland; we can obtain some glimpse of it within the area where the sound changes are generated.

The Geographic Reversal

The preceding discussion of language and politics shows a remarkable reversal of political geography in the Republican/Democratic opposition. The Democratic orientation of the Inland North is something new; in fact, we saw earlier that the most active ideologists of the Northern evangelicals flooded into the Republican Party, not the Democratic Party. The startling reversal of the parties' geographic base is shown in table 8.

The last four lines of the table note set up four groups of states, based on the predominant dialect pattern: S[outh], M[idland], N[ew] E[ngland], and N[orth]. The states taken to represent the North are limited to those where most of the area falls into the Northern dialect

Table 8 Presidential elections by four state groups of the eastern United States

		S	M	NE	N	
1848	Fillmore	/	/	/	/	Whig vs. D
1852	Pierce	(D)	D	/	D	Republican Party formed
1856	Buchanan	D	(D)	R	R	
1860	Lincoln	D	(R)	R	R	
1864	Lincoln	S	(R)	R	R	S = Confederate States
1868–76	Johnson/Grant/Hayes			Reconstruction		
1880	Garfield	D	/	R	R	
1884	Cleveland	D	/	(R)	(R)	
1888	Harrison	D	/	(R)	R	
1892	Cleveland	D	/	(R)	/	
1896	McKinley	D	(R)	R	R	
1900	McKinley	D	(R)	R	R	
1904	Roosevelt	D	R	R	R	
1908	Taft	D	R	R	R	
1912	Wilson	D	(D)	(D)	(D)	Progressive 3rd party
1916	Wilson	D	/	(R)	R	
1920	Harding	(D)	R	R	R	
1924	Coolidge	D	R	R	R	
1928	Hoover	/	R	R	R	S core D: AR, LA, MI, AL, GA, SC
1932	Roosevelt	D	/	(R)	D	NE core R: ME, VT
1936	Roosevelt	D	D	/	D	NE core R: ME, VT
1940	Roosevelt	D	(D)	/	(D)	NE core R: ME, VT
1944	Roosevelt	D	/	/	/	NE core R: ME, VT
1948	Truman	/	/	(R)	/	States Rights: LA, MI, AL, SC
1952	Eisenhower	/	R	R	R	S core D: LA, MI, AL ,GA, SC, NC
1956	Eisenhower	/	R	R	R	S core D: AR, MI, AL, GA, SC, NC
1960	Kennedy	/	/	/	/	Electors for Byrd in AL, MI
1964	Johnson	/	D	D	D	S core R: LA, MI, AL, GA, SC
1968	Nixon	W	/	/	/	Wallace (Ind): LA, AR, MI, AL, GA
1972	Nixon	R	R	(R)	R	
1976	Carter	(D)	/	/	/	R: VA
1980	Reagan	(R)	/	R	(R)	
1984	Reagan	R	R	R	(R)	
1988	Bush	R	(R)	/	(D)	
1992	Clinton	/	(D)	D	D	S core R: MI, AL, FL, SC, NC, VA
1996	Clinton	/	(D)	D	D	S core R: MI, AL, GA, SC, NC, VA
2000	Bush	R	/	(D)	D	NE core R: NH
2004	Bush	R	/	D	D	
2008	Obama	/	/	D	D	S core R: [TX], AK, LA, MI, AL, GA, SC

Note:

D = Democrat; R = Republican; (X) = one state deviant; / = 2+ states deviant
S[outh] = TX, AR, LA, MS, AL, GA, FL, SC, NC, KY, TN, VA
M[idland] = MO, IL, IN, OH, WV, PA, DE, MD, NJ
N[ew] E[ngland] = ME, VT, NH, MA, RI, CT
N[orth] = NY, MI, WI, IA, MN

region: New York, Michigan, Wisconsin, Iowa, and Minnesota, so that the Northern orientation of the upper third of Illinois and Ohio is not represented here. On the other hand, the states representing the South fall almost entirely within the boundary that defines the Southern dialect region in the *Atlas of North American English*.[2]

Each successive line shows the predominant voting pattern for that presidential election, where a D or an R means solidly Democratic or Republican, (D) or (R) the same result with one state deviant, and / stands for a split with more than one state deviating from the main trend. The main focus will be on the S and N columns, which oppose most directly the South and the North.

The first line of table 8 displays the Whig vs. Democrat election of 1848, before the Republican Party was formed. The Democrats did not control the South then, but their control of that region began in the following election and continued without a break for 92 years—except for the period of Reconstruction after the war, when Republican governments were supported by federal troops. Though the Republican sweep of 1928 dented the Democratic monopoly of the South, it did not disturb the six core southern states. The series of D symbols in the Southern column comes to an end in the election of 1948, when southern opposition to Truman's civil rights platform created a "States Rights" third party. The Republican domination of the North was almost as consistent from 1856 through 1928. The period 1928 to 1988 is marked by many fluctuations. One of the crucial developments in political ideology was the New Deal policies of the Roosevelt years of 1932 on, when the Democratic Party moved strongly into what had been the basic Republican position: that federal activism could advance economic and social welfare. Nevertheless, we note during this period that there remained a New England core of Maine and Vermont that voted consistently Republican during these years. It was not until the Clinton election of 1992 that the North voted solidly Democratic. The remarkable geographic reversal of political parties was complete by 2000 and 2004, and we have the crystallization of the Republican domination of the South, in the face of an opposing Democratic block in the North.

The earlier sections of this chapter documented the ways in which the Yankee evangelical antislavery movement formed the core of the

Republican Party in its early stages. How do we account for the transformation that realigned the same Yankee settlement and dialect area with the Blue State Democrats? A suggestive line of inquiry follows the continuing history of attitudes toward and legislation dealing with racial inequality in the United States.

Table 8 shows that the Democratic control of the South was shattered from 1948 on with the formation of a states' rights movement in opposition to growing northern pressure in support of the civil rights movement. A crucial change in the orientation of the two parties was the election of 1964 after Johnson shepherded the Civil Rights Act through Congress. The Republican Party was not opposed to this legislation: the vote split on regional lines, not party lines. Among northern Republicans, the great majority voted for the bill, 138 to 24 against.

One of Johnson's most effective arguments was that passing this legislation was "the late president's most fitting memorial" (Beschloss 2007, 279). In fact, Kennedy was for a long time ambivalent in his support of the Civil Rights Act, which he postponed many times, mindful of losing the southern vote that had elected him. In a recorded conversation with Louisiana Senator Russell Long,[3] Kennedy learned of an offer by segregationists to exchange their electoral votes for abandonment of the civil rights legislation, as in the deal that led to the end of Reconstruction under Rutherford Hayes in 1876. JFK responded,

> But this isn't 1876. Because what happens is it will become the most publicized thing . . . everybody's looking, now what is this president promising this group and pretty soon you've got the Goddamndest mayhem.

Long suggested that "the Negro vote might be the key vote," and JFK replied:

> At least I could count it . . . I think it's crazy for the South because this way I'm concerned about Georgia and Louisiana and these places, here's where we got a chance to carry them, but if I end up with no chance to carry them then I gotta go up *north* and try to do my business.

The Johnson election that followed showed the first switch of the core southern states (Louisiana, Mississippi, Alabama, Georgia, and

South Carolina) to the Republican column, and the first Democratic vote in the North since Roosevelt. It is not unreasonable to say that the current realignment of Red States vs. Blue States was a consequence of the political strategy that initiated the Civil Rights Act of 1964 and the Voting Rights Act of 1965.

The common thread that unites this history of 150 years is the attitudes of whites toward slavery and the inequality of blacks and whites in the United States. In the North, both abolitionists and moderates, formalists and antiformalists, pietists and liturgicals, shared the common articles of faith that all men were created equal, that slavery was a sin. A century and a half later, this ideology was the moving force that led to the coincidence of the Inland North dialect and the political stance of the Blue States. As Carwardine points out, the cultural style of the Yankee evangelical movement resembled that of modern-day Far Right revivalists. However, the cultural content differed on the crucial dimension of race relations. In the latest election of 2008, the solid core of the Democratic majority is expanded, but the Northern dialect region remains solidly Democratic.

The question posed by this chapter may then be restated. Does the continuation of Yankee ideology seen in this political and geographic reversal also contribute to the momentum exhibited by the Northern Cities Shift across the Inland North?

The major theme of this book is the effort to account for the growing divergence of regional dialects in North America, The reader will have observed that race is a recurring theme throughout, in expected and unexpected ways. In one form or another, the politics of America are the politics of race: it is hard to believe that any major social change can take place in America without some correlation with race and racial issues. The long history of slavery and racial inequality has left an indelible stamp on Americans' view of human identity. The sound change on Martha's Vineyard seemed to have nothing to do with race; yet racial thinking was always ready to emerge. When I asked about the Indians of Gay Head, I was told by some that they weren't really Indians, just "no-account people" who had intermarried with blacks.[1] In New York City, I originally attributed the retreat from r-lessness to a decline of the prestige of Britain and British pronunciation. Yet Bonfiglio (2002) has made a substantial argument that the driving force against r-less pronunciation is its association with African American speech. In South Harlem, I studied the effects of rising racial segregation, itself an exploitation of racial prejudice through redlining and blockbusting. I also observed a correlation of AAVE with the converse development of racial pride, as the Cobras were transformed into the Bohemian Brothers through their association with the Nation of Islam, with a rich ideology of race-centered African history.

We could speculate on the internal forces that are driving the new developments in African American Vernacular English. These explanations must be found in a frontier area of semantic theory, where principles of linguistic change are not well developed. But the forces that are driving AAVE away from other dialects are easier to identify. This withdrawal carries its own dynamics. What we saw in Philadelphia is that a single step of entry into the white dialect—saying [hæos] instead of [haos]—was equivalent to a change in ethnicity, a paradigmatic case of "acting white," and a behavior that is highly criticized within the black community. The radical sound changes that are operating in North America continue to separate black and white speech. Studies of African Americans in Northern Cities Shift cities show only limited adaptation to the vowel systems of the surrounding communities. In each major city, we can observe an increase of racial differences in language over time as African Americans and Latinos maintain their distance from these new creations of the white majority. Even in the South, where the AAVE sound system originated, we observe that African Americans are differentiated from whites in their conservative participation in Southern sound changes.

At one point I formed the hypothesis that the driving force behind the new sound changes in the mainstream might be the pressure on whites to keep their distance from blacks, as in Bonfiglio's hypothesis on the decline of r-lessness. If so, one would find that the rate of change was proportional to the degree of black/white tension. This proved not to be so. The development of the Northern Cities Shift is uniform in every major city of the Inland North.

Consider the linguistic situation that emerged in chapter 7 from the point of view of an African American growing up in Chicago. It seemed possible that the Northern Cities Shift is associated with liberal attitudes toward race, an association continued from the abolitionist cause over a century and a half ago. Let us assume for the moment that it is unconsciously perceived by African Americans as being so. What then has been accomplished by this movement? Does it reach so far into the life chances of black youth that they are free to engage in the new phonetic practices that they hear around them? From one point of view, the abolitionist cause has triumphed: slavery is abolished, and African Americans have successfully led the struggle for civil rights that has enabled great numbers to advance their position in American society. But for the majority who remain in the inner city this is an ideological change, not a substantial one. Mass unemployment, mass incarceration, and mass educational failure are the reality facing children as they emerge from the local schools. Everyday life brings home the distinction, over and over again, between how things are supposed to be and how they are.

There can be no doubt that the Northern Cities Shift is a white phenomenon. Let us now consider it from the standpoint of the white majority, following paths of phonetic development that carry them further away from the speech of their parents and the speech of other regions as well. This returns us to the initial questions about language change that followed from an examination of misunderstandings in everyday life. If language evolved as an instrument of communication, what evolutionary forces are responsible for the ongoing changes that limit communication? We considered the early evidence that we are territorial animals, with a need to mark our local territory as different from others. But when dialect geography reaches continental proportions, we have to look beyond local identity for social correlates of equivalent dimensions. We extended our explorations to large-scale cultural constructs in the domains of religion, race, and politics. Yet it must be emphasized that the evidence for such motivating factors is mainly correlational: the mechanism by which cultural patterns drive language change remains mysterious.

The Firm Hand of the Past and the Doctrine of First Effective Settlement

The previous chapter traced an association of dialect development with the political orientation of the original Yankee settlers. Yet only a small minority of the speakers of the Inland North are now of Yankee descent. The *Atlas* policy was to select from the telephone book representatives of the dominant ethnic group in each city. In many sections of the North and Midland, German ancestry predominates among the speakers whose vowel systems we studied, with a good representation from other European countries. We see here the cultural and linguistic realization of the Doctrine of First Effective Settlement, as developed by Zelinsky (1992): that is, the first settlers in a community set the cultural pattern that is followed by successive waves of immigrants, no matter how numerous they may be. In our sociolinguistic studies, we have demonstrated that second-generation Americans are fully representative of the local dialect of third-, fourth-, and eighth-generation Americans. We have found that the leaders of sound change are young women from the second and third generation of newly arrived ethnic groups. Now we may ask, what are the critical cultural configurations that have been absorbed by these children of German or Polish immigrants to Detroit, Michigan, as opposed to the patterns learned by the children of German or Polish immigrants to Columbus, Ohio?

On the one hand, we have to remember that political and cultural differences across the North/Midland line are small, and in the long history of presidential elections, most are decided by small majorities. The same can be said for the long history of contest between Republicans and Democrats near the North/Midland boundary. Table 9 illustrates the struggle between these parties in Indiana from 1880 to 1896, taken from Jensen (1971). The statewide vote is very close to 50% throughout. Yet note that the 19 counties classed as "urban and Yankee" were consistently more Republican than any others by small margins, and when their percentage rose to 54%, 52%, 53%, 55%, and 55%, it tipped the statewide balance. This is the same mathematics that we saw operating in the Bush/Kerry election, but on the other side of the North/South reversal in Republican politics.

On the other hand, we observe the grim history of segregated schools and concentrated poverty in these same Northern cities that were swept by religious enthusiasm in opposition to slavery. If there is an association of northern liberal attitudes toward race and North-

Table 9 Percentage of popular vote for the Republican Party in Indiana by county type and Yankee origin, 1880–96

County category	1880	1884	1886	1888	1890	1892	1894	1896
49 most rural	48	47	48	48	45	45	49	49
43 most urban	50	49	49	49	45	46	51	53
19 urban and Yankee	54	53	52	53	49	50	55	55
24 urban and non-Yankee	48	46	47	47	42	44	49	51
Statewide	49	48	49	49	45	46	50	51
Winner	Rep.	Dem.	Rep.	Rep.	Dem.	Dem.	Rep.	Rep.

Source: Jensen 1971.

ern dialect it does not mean that racism is not characteristic of these northern cities as it is in the South. There is no shortage of racists in the Inland North. It must be admitted that despite the great effect on public consciousness brought about by the election of President Obama, the shift we see in this country is largely a shift in public discourse: what views are proper to express in public, what words can or cannot be used to express racial prejudice.

Nevertheless, there is a continuity in the American commitment to fairness and equality, and there is a movement to make that commitment more real. The northern settlement area continues to lead in that direction, and I propose that one of the historical forces behind language change is the ideology inherited from the original Yankee settlers. With all their meddlesome and cantankerous ways, the Yankee community had a deep-seated commitment to making this world a better place. If there is a social motivation to the Northern Cities Shift, it is interesting to think that it might be connected with the better part of our human nature.

Appendix

Summary Statement on African American Vernacular English

Submitted by Nine Linguists to the California Curriculum Commission on February 10, 2008

The following statement is grounded in current knowledge of African American Vernacular English concentrating on those aspects that have the most relevance to the acquisition of standard academic English reading and writing in the classroom. We have written it in response to the new criterion in the California Curriculum Commission 2008 K–8 Reading/Language Arts/English Language Arts Criteria, adopted April 17, 2006, which requires:

> . . . additional support for students who use African American Vernacular English who may have difficulty with phonological awareness and standard academic English structures of oral and written language, including spelling and grammar. (p. 456)

The range of linguistic research on the language of the African American community conducted by the authors dates from the 1960s to the present. Although there is wide variation in the use of English across the African American community, our description concentrates on African American Vernacular English [AAVE], the linguistic system used by and among many African Americans in every-day life. Throughout more than one hundred years of research conducted on this linguistic phenomenon, scholars, including the authors of this document, have given it a variety of names. Here we shall use the terminology employed in the California Curriculum Commission Adoption Criteria: "African American Vernacular English" (AAVE). Our hope is that this knowledge will be used to ensure that all children, regardless of social, ethnic, or linguistic background, have the ability to read and to write English in ways that lead to academic success.

There are still many areas of disagreement on the origin and past history of AAVE and there are many open questions concerning the current direction of its development. However, there is general agreement on the main sound patterns and grammatical features that distinguish this variety from other dialects of English. These features have often been found to be similar across the United States in areas with a high degree of residential segregation, and are represented in the language of African American children with great regularity, particularly in schools in low socioeconomic areas with a high concentration of African Americans. There is also general agreement that the goal for African American students should be additive, not subtractive: that is, learning standard academic English, without a focus on eliminating AAVE.

Because AAVE is a language system with well-formed rules for sounds, grammar and meanings, teachers can help children whose speech follows these rules to learn standard academic English if they receive special practice at just those points where their language differs from the standard.

While there are numerous patterns that are unique to AAVE, an exhaustive account is beyond the scope of this summary, which concentrates on those patterns that have the most immediate effect on reading and writing. The crucial point is that these patterns do not form a list of separate items, but rather combine to reinforce each other. The sound patterns described in (I) below intersect in many ways with the grammatical patterns in (II). Those interested in a comprehensive, detailed description of AAVE are referred to the references attached to this summary. The most complete published account of AAVE features is to be found in J. R. Rickford, *African American Vernacular English: Features and Use, Evolution, and Educational Implications*. Oxford: Blackwell, 1999.

I. Sounds

/th/

The initial *th-* in function words *this, then, these, other, either,* etc. is often produced as a rapidly spoken /d/, and less often like a /t/ in content words like *thing, think, through.*

At the ends of words or syllables, many speakers of AAVE use the sound /f/ for both *-th* and *-f,* so that *bathroom* is pronounced as *bafroom* and *death* as *deaf.* Moreover, many speakers of AAVE do not hear the difference between the two sounds.

This also applies to the consonant spelled *th* in the middle and ends of words, as in *brother* and *breathe,* which is frequently pronounced with a /v/.

The *th* words pose more of a problem for learning to spell and speak standard academic English than for learning to read.

Pronunciation of /r/

The main regional feature of AAVE concerns the pronunciation of /r/. In the high prestige pronunciation of southern England, the sound spelled *r* after a vowel is normally pronounced as a continuation of the vowel, so that *father* and *farther, source* and *sauce* are alike. This vowel-like pronunciation was also the prestige pronunciation in Boston, New York, Richmond, Charleston and Savannah, but shortly after World War II, people in these cities began to pronounce /r/ as a consonant in careful speech, as in other parts of the U.S. In all these cities and elsewhere, African Americans use the vowel-like pronunciation of /r/ more than Whites, not only at the ends of words, but also between two vowels, as in *Flo'ida, Ca'olina, inte'ested,* etc. In cities with *r*-less dialects like New York, speakers of AAVE show much more of this pattern than in *r*-pronouncing cities like Chicago. As in Southern varieties, AAVE may eliminate all traces of the vowel that represented /r/ in words like *sto', do', fo'* which sound like *stow, foe, dough* instead of *store, door, four.*

Among the consonant clusters at the beginning of the word, AAVE frequently shows the absence of /r/, as in the words *throw, through, brought,* often pronounced *th'ow, th'ough, b'ought.*

The general tendency in AAVE as elsewhere is for speakers with r-less pronunciation to pronounce /r/ as a consonant in formal speech. Whether or not speakers of AAVE acquire the pronunciation of /r/ at the ends of words, they should become aware of which words are spelled with r (i.e., *snore*) and which are not (*snow*).

Pronunciation of /l/

As in several other varieties, AAVE speakers pronounce /l/ with a vowel-like quality at the ends of words, particularly after the vowels of *cool* and *coal*. This is most frequent before the consonants /p, t, k/ and therefore it is difficult for AAVE speakers to develop phonemic awareness of the next to last segment in *help, belt, milk,* and such words are often spelled without /l/ by AAVE-speaking students. Final *-le,* as in *people, couple* and *little,* is often produced as an /u/ vowel.

Consonant Clusters

All English speakers show some tendency to omit the second of two consonants in words like *fist, wild, find, desk, lift,* especially when the next word begins with a consonant. Speakers of AAVE omit the second consonant at a higher rate than speakers of other varieties, and show a much greater tendency in sentence final position (*This is a test.*), where other varieties tend to preserve the /t/. When the -s of the plural is added (*tests, wasps, desks*) the combination of three consonants is rarely produced; *tests* is realized as *tes'* or *tesses.*

As a result of this process, AAVE speakers may produce and hear as homonyms *miss* and *mist, cold* and *coal, find* and *fine.* Given the vowel-like pronunciation of /l/, one can have even larger sets of homonyms, so that *bow = bowl = bold.* When a vowel follows, the second consonant is much more likely to be produced and heard. This is especially true within a word, so that the final /t/ of *test* is most likely to appear in *testing,* and the final /t/ of *accept* even more likely to appear in *acceptable.*

The situation is quite different for the consonant combinations *-mp, -nt, -nk, -lp, -lt, -lk,* where it is the first consonant that tends to be weakened and is hard to hear.

A prominent sound pattern of AAVE is the absence of the /t/ in the common words *it's, that's, lots, what's,* so that these words sound like *i's, tha's, lo's* and *wha's.*

Speakers of AAVE from some regions of the South use initial /skr/ in place of /str/ so that *street* is pronounced like *skreet.*

/i/ and /e/ before /m/ and /n/

As in the South generally, speakers of AAVE do not make a difference between /i/ and /e/ before the nasal consonants /m/ and /n/, so that *pin* and *pen, him* and *hem* sound the same. Most of the time the vowel will sound like *-in* for both words, but sometimes *-en* will be used for both. Many speakers of AAVE do not hear a difference between /i/ and /e/ in these words. This type of pronunciation is heard among most educated speakers in the South, Black and White, who are not speakers of AAVE.

Words spelled with *-ing* are often pronounced with the vowel of *-ang,* so that words like *thing, sing, ring* may have the vowel of *thang, sang, rang.* This pronunciation is common in the South, and generally considered nonstandard.

II. Grammar

The Verb System

Subject-Verb Agreement

In the present tense of Standard academic English, a suffix *-s* is added to the verb if the subject is in the third person (*he, she, it* . . .). In AAVE, this suffix is most often absent, and there is no consistent difference between the third person and other persons. The main agreement of subject and verb is found in the verb *to be: I am, you are, he/she/it is* . . . In speech, the *-s* will sometimes appear in other places (*we goes there; He can gets hurt*). To acquire standard academic English speech and writing, speakers of AAVE have to learn to use *-s* with the third person and only there.

The regular agreement of subject and verb is also missing for the irregular verbs *does/do, have/has* and *was/were.* In AAVE, forms produced are most often *do, have* and *was.*

The Past Tense

Standard academic English forms the past tense of regular verbs with the suffix -ed, which usually forms a consonant combination or cluster in verbs like *worked* or *rolled* (but not in *started*). In pronunciation, these -ed suffixes form clusters of consonants (/kt, ld/). Like other consonant clusters (see page one), this combination can be simplified, but less often than clusters that form part of the basic word (*fist, hand*). In speech, in AAVE, the second consonant is deleted more often than in other varieties, so that the past can sound the same as the present. In speech, the past sometimes is realized with two consonants (*pickted*), and this happens very often in reading, when struggling readers are trying hard to pronounce past tense verbs. This and other evidence indicates that speakers of AAVE usually understand the past tense meaning of -ed, whether or not they pronounce it. However, it is sometimes omitted in writing, and AAVE speakers have to learn when and where to use it in writing standard academic English.

AAVE can also mark the simple past tense with the auxiliary *had*, which always indicates the past perfect in standard academic English.

Standard academic English has a past perfect form, *John had told me that*, which indicates that John had told me the information at some time previous to the time being talked about. In AAVE, the past with *had* is often used to mean the simple past, so that *John had told me that* means the same as *John told me that*.

As noted above, the past tense of *be* is regularly *was*.

Like many other varieties, AAVE has many nonstandard forms of irregular verbs for the simple past and the past participle, as in *He seen that* and *He had ran over there*.

The Verb to Be

In the first person present, AAVE uses *I am* or *I'm* like other varieties, but often sounds like "Uhm."

AAVE can have the full forms *are* or *is*, the contracted forms *'re* or *'s*, or no form at all (*We are coming, we're coming, we coming; he is going, he's going, he going*). Wherever Standard academic English can use contractions, AAVE can have either contraction or nothing at all. The frequency of the "zero" form varies, less often with nouns (*He my brother*) and more often with verbs (*She goin' over there*). Children who speak AAVE often have difficulty with contracted forms, and find the uncontracted forms easier to read. To master Standard academic English, AAVE speakers have to learn to produce consistently, either the full forms *is* and *are,* or the contracted *'s* and *'re.*

This variation is not found when *is* or *are* receive stress, as in *That's what he is,* or *Is he coming?* or *Yes he is.*

After *it, that* and *what, is* is fused with the /t/, as noted in the discussion of existential constructions below.

The complete omission of the verb *to be* is not found in the past tense, whereas *was* is rarely deleted. But *was* very often appears in the plural as well as the singular, giving forms such as *They was* as well as *He was.*

AAVE frequently uses an invariant form of the verb *to be* to indicate habitual action (*He always be doing this*). To master Standard academic English, speakers of AAVE must learn to avoid this form in favor of *am, are* or *is.* Moreover, practice is needed in placing these words before the adverbs *always, never,* etc. rather than after (*He is always doing this* instead of *He always is doing this*).

The Possessive System

In Standard academic English, *'s* is added to a noun to indicate possession, as in *John's cat* and *This is John's.* In AAVE, the *'s* suffix is normally absent when another noun follows (*John cat*) but it does appear when there is no noun (*This is John's.*) The possessive *'s* is also regularly added to *mine* (*This is mines*).

The possessive pronoun *whose* is not usually found in AAVE, but is realized as *who* (*I don't know who book it was*).

To acquire standard academic English, speakers of AAVE must learn to recognize and reproduce the *'s* marker of possession between two nouns.

Existential Constructions

AAVE has a number of ways of expressing 'existence,' but we will focus here on the use of *it.* Like other Southern varieties, AAVE uses *it* in existential sentences, "It's a man at the door," where standard academic English uses *There* ("There's a man at the door"). As with standard academic English, the contracted verb is normally singular. This grammatical difference combines with the AAVE reduction of consonant clusters, so there are three forms pronounced [Is]:

1. existential *it,* as in "It's a whole lotta people birfday today."
2. possessive *its,* as in "The lil bird hurt its lil wing."
3. contracted form of *it is,* as in "The present I got, it's big."

The AAVE-speaking child will need help in the pronunciation of *its* in standard academic English, as well as help in expressing existential type sentences in standard academic English, using the patterns *there is/there are.* In writing, the child will need help learning how to represent the contraction *it's* and help distinguishing the contracted form *it's* from the possessive form *its.*

The Plural Marking System

AAVE uses the plural *-s,* except when numbers occur with the "nouns of measure" (*It cost five dollar, she owe me thirty cent.*) This is also a regional feature of Southern colloquial speech. However, the plural /s/ is often observed to be absent in the writing of AAVE speakers, and practice in this feature of standard academic English can be helpful.

When the plural /s/ is added to a stem ending in /st/, the /t/ either disappears, is omitted or is replaced by an unstressed vowel (*tests* is realized as *tess* or *tesses*).

The Negative System

Many nonstandard varieties of English use several negatives in a sentence where a single negative meaning is intended (*Nobody never said nothing*). The additional negatives with *no, never, neither,* appear where standard academic English uses *any, ever* and *either.* In AAVE, this pattern is almost 100%, and follows the logic that is most common in languages of the world including French and Spanish, where negatives reinforce rather than cancel each other. This pattern is often combined with the foregrounding of the negative (as in Southern colloquial speech), giving *Can't nobody do that* as an emphatic way of saying *Nobody can do that.*

To master the writing and speaking of standard academic English, users of AAVE need considerable practice to gain control of *any, ever* and *either* after a negative word.

Socio-cultural Attitudes

In addition to linguistic patterns and features that impact language and literacy learning for AAVE-speaking children in K–8 classrooms, socio-cultural perspectives and attitudes need to be taken into consideration, particularly the attitudes of middle school students in grades 5/6–8. Some AAVE-speaking students approaching adolescence exhibit resistance to and/or skepticism about the value of learning standard academic English. Some students may need support to learn that it is possible to acquire mastery of standard academic English without rejecting the language used by their parents in the home. The students in these grades will need help in understanding that what is appropriate in one setting is not appropriate in another, so that they can shift easily and competently between varieties in all different social contexts.

Although linguists may sometimes disagree about the historical development of AAVE and its current direction of development, it is generally accepted that AAVE is the rule-governed system described above. If appropriate methods are used in the classroom, children who speak this variety can achieve the goal of mastering standard academic English. Such instruction will be all the more effective if it identifies nonstandard varieties as different, rather than inferior. All students (regardless of linguistic, social, and economic background) should be taught standard academic English in a way that respects the richness, legitimacy, and vitality of their home language.

(signed)

WILLIAM LABOV, Professor and Director of the Linguistics
    Laboratory, University of Pennsylvania
H. SAMY ALIM, Assistant Professor of Anthropology, UCLA
GUY BAILEY, Chancellor, University of Missouri–Kansas City
JOHN BAUGH, Professor, Director of African and African American
    Studies, Washington University in St. Louis
ANNE H. CHARITY, Assistant Professor of English and Linguistics,
    The College of William and Mary in Williamsburg, Virginia
LISA J. GREEN, Associate Professor of Linguistics, University of
    Massachusetts, Amherst

John R. Rickford, Professor of Linguistics, Stanford University
Tracey Weldon, Associate Professor, English Language and
   Literature, University of South Carolina
Walt Wolfram, William C. Friday Distinguished Professor,
   Department of English, North Carolina State University

Notes

1. About Language and Language Change

1. Entry dated July 26, 2006, http://www.alphadictionary.com/blog/?p=15 (accessed November 11, 2011).

2. The apostrophe signals that the nasal consonant is made with apical contact of the tongue against the gum ridge, while the -ng spelling indicates a velar contact with the back of the tongue against the soft palate. In phonetic notation, this is [gʊdmɔrnɪn] vs. [gʊdmɔrnɪŋ]. In everyday speech, this variation is usually called "dropping the g."

3. For a description of these methods, see Labov 1966b, 1984. But with this proviso: these methods are only useful when we are studying very frequent phenomena. It is not useful for many questions in syntax and semantics, which have to draw on examples that rarely occur in speech. As in other fields, there is no one way to skin a cat in linguistics.

4. See Chomsky 1986 for an early definition of universal grammar.

2. A Hidden Consensus

1. The original study (Labov 1966b) was republished in a second edition in 2006 with extensive additions.

2. The definition of this variable—the set of words in which both -in' and -ing are possible—is not a simple matter. It includes the verb working and the noun ceiling; it does not include the word thing but it does include nothing and something; it includes the verb flushing but not Flushing, Long Island.

3. For a partial catalog of these results, see the final chapter of the second edition of Labov 1966b [2006].

4. See http://www.balleralert.com/forum/topics/president-obamas-fathers-day.

5. See Fischer 1958 for New England; Trudgill 1974 for Norwich, England; Bradley and Bradley 1979 for Melbourne, Australia; Cofer 1972 for Philadelphia; Houston 1991 for 20 cities in England; Douglas-Cowie 1978 for Northern Ireland; Mock 1979 for rural Missouri.

6. As noted at the beginning, *-in'* descends from an Old English noun ending, and *-ing* from a verbal ending. The historical reflex is seen in the fact that everyone uses more *-ing* in nouns and more *-in'* in verbs, though this is hidden from social consciousness and carries no social meaning.

3. Hidden Diversity

1. The Midland area (to be defined below) shows the use of positive *anymore* in sentences like, "Cars are sure expensive anymore"; of *swept* in place of *sweeping*, as in "The floor needs swept." The South shows a wide range of grammatical features, including double modals, in "He might could do that," or negative inversion, in "Can't nobody do that." But none of these and other grammatical variables have been found to be involved in large-scale and systematic expansion, like the sound changes to be discussed in this chapter.

2. These observations were first reported in Labov, Yaeger, and Steiner 1972, the first large-scale application of acoustic measurement to the study of linguistic change.

3. This research project at the University of Pennsylvania was supported by the National Science Foundation and reported in chapters 2–4 of Labov 2010a.

4. For many readers of this chapter this will sound like nonsense. The two word classes involved, in *cod* and *cawed, hock* and *hawk, Don* and *dawn*, have long since merged for them and are pronounced the same. This applies to readers who were raised in Canada, eastern New England, western Pennsylvania, and the West generally. But in the North, the mid-Atlantic states, and most of the South, *cod* and *cawed* are not the same; short-o and "long open-o" are two distinct categories.

5. I am grateful to Suzanne Evans Wagner, the linguist in question, for these observations.

6. The same profile was drawn in a study of a very different society, in an investigation of linguistic change in Cairo, Egypt, by Niloofar Haeri (1996).

7. The earliest evidence for the first two stages of the NCS appeared in an unpublished paper by Fasold (1969), based on the sociolinguistic study of Detroit by Shuy, Wolfram, and Riley (1967). Fasold reported that lower-middle-class white females led in the fronting of short-a, short-o, and long open-o.

8. Note that in figure 8, the Midland is broken in two by a narrow strip running from Chicago down to St Louis, representing the influence of Chicago speech patterns on that city (Labov 2007).

9. One essential condition is the preservation of the distinction between short-o in *got* and long open-o in *bought*, so that *don* and *dawn, cot* and *caught, collar* and *caller,* are all different. If short-o moves back to merge with long open-o, the Northern Cities Shift is no longer a possibility.

10. See maps 14.4–9 of the *Atlas of North American English.*

11. Nevertheless, impressionistic phonetic judgments play an essential role in the study of sound change, since the more precise acoustic measurements are also subject to gross errors in the identification of the first and second formants, and here judgments made by ear serve to control and correct such errors.

12. The outer boundaries of points that satisfy these other measures are shown in figure 10 as well. These are:

    AE1: A measure of the raising of short-a: short-a is in upper mid position (F1 less than 700 Hz).

    EQ: Reversal of the relative positions of short-a and short-e: short-a is higher and fronter than short-e.

    ED: Approximation of short-e and short-o on the front-back dimension: the F2 difference between them is less than 375 Hz.

13. This "St. Louis corridor" traces the influence of the Chicago Northern Cities Shift on St. Louis. See Labov 2007 for the history of this influence along Route I-55, the forerunner of fabled Route 66.

14. Brockmann's computational model is best known for its use in tracking and predicting the spread of the swine flu epidemic (*New York Times,* May 3, 2009, http://www.nytimes.com/2009/05/04/health/04model.html?_r=1). The communication patterns that emerge from the dollar-bill flux are very similar to those produced by studies of airline traffic by Alessandro Vespignani of Indiana University.

4. The Growing Divergence of Black and White English

1. See Labov and Harris 1986; Ash and Myhill 1986; Graff, Labov, and Harris 1986.

2. The contracted form of the verb *is* as *'s* is technically a *clitic,* but like a suffix, it is less than a word.

3. See Labov 1969a and 1972 for the analysis of the underlying status of the copula and past tense forms.

4. Excluding those whose speech did not include any third singular tokens.

5. The classic demonstration of how variables align to community norms as the data set increases is Guy's 1980 study of -t,d deletion.

6. Here "flicted" is derived from "conflicted" or maybe "afflicted," a term commonly used in jump rope for "twisted."

7. By far the largest body of data on AAVE tense and aspect is the product of Dayton's 1996 dissertation. Dayton did no audio recording, but wrote down her examples in the course of four years' fieldwork among social networks in the AAVE community of West Philadelphia.

8. The use of capitals for BE DONE should not be taken to mean stress. Unlike stressed BIN, BE DONE is a rapid and reduced form, and may not even be noticed by a listener who speaks another dialect.

9. The U.S. Census shows dissimilarity indices for the Philadelphia metropolitan area as .781 for 1980, .768 for 1990, and .720 for 2000.

10. The findings of the *Atlas* that are central to this book provide one large body of evidence for this point. More general support is derived from social learning theory (Bandura 1977) and the role of social interaction in learning as developed by Vygotsky (Forman and Cazden 1985).

5. The Politics of African American English

1. Following the 1971 Supreme Court ruling *Swann v. Charlotte-Mecklenburg Board of Education,* many states instituted mandatory busing to reduce segregation in public schools. These programs have largely disappeared and did not affect the ethnic composition of the schools in which the reading problems discussed in this chapter were observed.

2. The most convincing experiments that demonstrate this effect were carried out by Seligman, Tucker, and Lambert in Montreal in 1972. They obtained drawings, writings, photos, and speech samples from Montreal schoolchildren and then asked student teachers to rate them. They then put together combinations of the best- and the worst-rated drawing, writing, photography, and speech, and asked other student teachers to rate these composite individuals. The use of nonstandard Montreal French (Quebecois) had much the greatest effect on judgments of intelligence and likelihood of success in school.

3. Including Jerrie Scott, Milford Jeremiah, Richard Bailey, J. L. Dillard, and myself. See Smitherman 1981 and Labov 1982b for a detailed account of this trial.

4. A timeline of the Ebonics controversy is available at http://www.pbs.org/speak/seatosea/americanvarieties/AAVE/timeline/ (accessed January 7, 2011). See also Baugh (2000).

5. Dated October 31, 1995. Accessed January 7, 2011, from http://econfaculty.gmu.edu/wew/articles/95/Black-English.htm.

6. See http://www.resist.com/ebonicsguide.htm.

7. See http://www.urbandictionary.com/define.php?term=ebonics (accessed January 7, 2011).

8. In our study of South Harlem (Labov et al. 1968), these tendencies are documented over several years. There are no records of the use of *has* by members of the named street groups.

9. I am drawing here on the many insights in Rickford and R. J. Rickford's treatment of humor in *Spoken Soul* (2000).

10. See http://media.www.theseahawk.org/media/storage/paper287/news/2010/03/03/News/Black.English.Creates.Controversy-3883025.shtm.

11. Other projects for creating dialect readers are reviewed by Rickford and A. E. Rickford (1996). See also Leaverton 1973.

12. A Bayesian Markov chain Monte Carlo model was used to take into account the frequency of the linguistic feature, the difficulty of the problem, and the

student's ability to do the problem. Of 10 characteristic variables of AAVE, 2 showed such effects most strongly: third singular -s and possessive -s.

6. Language Change as Local Politics

1. This pronunciation is not uncommon. It is often heard in Canada before voiceless consonants (*right, out,* but not in *ride, loud*) and is known among linguists as "Canadian raising." The same pattern was common in Virginia and is heard currently in Philadelphia (Labov 2001, chap. 4). In Martha's Vineyard, it was heard to some degree before all consonants, though strongest before the voiceless ones.

2. The following quotation from Donald Poole can be heard in the online publication (Labov 2009).

3. As in the extensive studies of the local dialect of the fishing community of Ocracoke on the Outer Banks of North Carolina by Wolfram and colleagues (Wolfram and Schilling-Estes 2004). See also Hazen 2002 for the contrast between local and extended identity in rural North Carolina.

4. The upper-class series was drawn from a series of interviews with 20 upperclass Philadelphians carried out by Anthony Kroch in coordination with the study of the other neighborhoods.

5. The linguist Ronald Kim reports a striking misunderstanding that dates back to the 1990s. He used to listen to a local rock station that frequently broadcast ads for a Philadelphia jewelry store that he understood as "Robbins Ethan Walnut," with the slogan "Our name is our address!" Over the years, he remembered "Ethan Walnut Street" as a strange address. In 1998 he was walking west on Walnut Street in Philadelphia's Old City, passed 8th Street, and saw the store with its sign reading "Robbins 8th and Walnut."

7. The Political Ideology of the Northern Cities Shift

1. The city dialects of Philadelphia and Pittsburgh were originally centers of the Midland dialect as defined in Kurath 1949, but their individual development was so distinctive that they are separate from the Midland in the *Atlas* treatment.

2. This dialect area is defined by the presence of glide deletion of the diphthong /ay/ in *my, time,* etc., as often spelled "mah," "tahm."

3. Played by Michael Beschloss during an interview with Terry Gross on NPR's *Fresh Air,* May 8, 2007, and summarized in Beschloss 2007.

8. Putting It All Together

1. Queequeg, of *Moby Dick,* was a Gay Head Indian. The Aquinnah Wampanoag tribe of Gay Head are the only Wampanoag tribe to have a formal land-in-trust reservation, and they participated in the successful Language Reclamation Project of the 1990s.

References

Ash, Sharon, and John Myhill. 1986. Linguistic correlates of inter-ethnic contact. In D. Sankoff (ed.), *Diversity and Diachrony*. Amsterdam and Philadelphia: John Benjamins. 33–44.

Atlas of North American English: Phonology and Sound Change. 2006. By William Labov, Sharon Ash, and Charles Boberg. Berlin: Mouton de Gruyter.

Bailey, Beryl. 1965. A new perspective on American Negro dialectology. *American Speech* 11:171–77.

Bailey, Guy. 1993. A perspective on African-American English. In Dennis Preston (ed.), *American Dialect Research*. Philadelphia: J. Benjamins. 287–318.

————. 2001. The relationship between African-American Vernacular English and white vernaculars in the American South. In Sonja Lanehart (ed.), *Sociocultural and Historical Contexts of African American English*. Philadelphia: J. Benjamins. 53–92.

Bailey, Guy, and Natalie Maynor. 1987. Decreolization? *Language in Society* 16:449–73.

Bailey, Guy, Natalie Maynor, and Patricia Cukor-Avila. 1991. *The Emergence of Black English: Text and Commentary*. Amsterdam and Philadelphia: J. Benjamins.

Bandura, Albert. 1977. *Social Learning Theory*. Englewood Cliffs, NJ: Prentice Hall.

Baranowski, Maciej. 2007. *Phonological Variation and Change in the Dialect of Charleston, South Carolina*. Publication of the American Dialect Society, 92. Durham: Duke Univ. Press.

Baugh, John. 1983. *Black Street Speech: Its History, Structure and Survival*. Austin: Univ. of Texas Press.

————. 2000. *Beyond Ebonics: Linguistic Pride and Racial Prejudice*. New York: Oxford Univ. Press.

Bereiter, Carl, and Siegfried Engelmann. 1966. *Teaching Disadvantaged Children in the Preschool*. Englewood Cliffs, NJ: Prentice-Hall.

Beschloss, Michael. 2007. *Presidential Courage*. New York: Simon and Schuster.

Blake, Renee, and Meredith Josey. 2003. The /ay/ diphthong in a Martha's Vineyard community: What can we say 40 years after Labov? *Language in Society* 32:451–85.

Bloomfield, Leonard. 1933. *Language*. New York: Henry Holt.

Boberg, Charles, and Stephanie M. Strassel. 2000. Short-a in Cincinnati: A change in progress. *Journal of English Linguistics* 28:108–26.

Bonfiglio, Thomas. 2002. *Race and the Rise of Standard American*. New York: Mouton de Gruyter, 2002.

Bradley, David, and Maya Bradley. 1979. *Melbourne Vowels*. Working Papers in Linguistics, 5. Melbourne: Linguistics Section, Univ. of Melbourne.

Butters, Ronald R. 1989. *The Death of Black English: Convergence and Divergence in Black and White Vernaculars*. Frankfurt: Peter Lang.

Carnes, Mark C., and John A. Garrity. 1996. *Mapping America's Past: A Historical Atlas*. New York: H. Holt.

Carver, Craig M. 1987. *American Regional Dialects: A Word Geography*. Ann Arbor: Univ. of Michigan Press.

Carwardine, Richard J. 1993. *Evangelicals and Politics in Antebellum America*. New Haven: Yale Univ. Press.

Charity, Anne H. 2007. Regional differences in low SES African-American children's speech in the school setting. *Language Variation and Change* 19:281–93.

Chomsky, Noam. 1986. *Knowledge of Language*. Cambridge, MA: MIT Press.

———. 1968. *Language and Mind*. New York: Harcourt, Brace & World.

Cofer, Thomas. 1972. Linguistic variability in a Philadelphia speech community. PhD diss., Univ. of Pennsylvania.

Conn, Jeffrey. 2005. Of "Moice" and men: The evolution of a male-led sound change. PhD diss., Univ. of Pennsylvania.

Cross, Whitney R. 1950. *The Burned-Over District: The Social and Intellectual History of Enthusiastic Religion in Western New York, 1800–1850*. Ithaca, NY: Cornell Univ. Press.

Cukor-Avila, Patricia. 1995. The evolution of AAVE in a rural Texas community: An ethnolinguistic study. PhD diss., Univ. of Michigan.

Darwin, Charles. 1871. *The Descent of Man, and Selection in Relation to Sex*. 1st ed. 2 vols. London: John Murray.

Dayton, Elizabeth. 1996. Grammatical categories of the verb in African American vernacular English. PhD diss., Univ. of Pennsylvania.

Dillard, J. L. 1973. The history of Black English. *Revista Interamericana/Interamerican Review* 2:507–20.

Douglas-Cowie, Ellen. 1978. Linguistic code-switching in a Northern Irish village: Social interaction and social ambition. In P. Trudgill (ed.), *Sociolinguistic Patterns in British English*. London: Edwin Arnold. 37–51.

Eckert, Penelope. 1989. *Jocks and Burnouts: Social Categories and Identities in the High School*. New York: Teachers College Press.

———. 2000. *Linguistic Variation as Social Practice*. Oxford: Blackwell.

Elazar, Daniel J. 1972. *American Federalism: A View from the States*. 2nd ed. New York: Thomas Y. Crowell.

Evans, Betsy E., Rika Ito, Jamila Jones, and Dennis R. Preston. 2006. How to get to be one kind of Midwesterner: Accommodation to the Northern Cities Chain Shift. In T. Murray and B. L. Simon (eds.), *Language Variation and Change in the American Midland*. Amsterdam: Benjamins, 179–97.

Fasold, Ralph. 1969. A sociolinguistic study of the pronunciation of three vowels in Detroit speech. Unpublished ms.

———. 1972. *Tense Marking in Black English*. Washington, DC: Center for Applied Linguistics.

———. 1976. One hundred years from syntax to phonology. In Sanford B. Steever, Carol A. Walker, and Salikoko S. Mufwene (eds.), *Papers from the Parasession on Diachronic Syntax, April 22, 1976*. Chicago: Chicago Linguistic Society.

Ferguson, Ann Arnett. 2001. *Bad Boys: Public Schools in the Making of Black Masculinity*. Ann Arbor: Univ. of Michigan Press.

Fischer, David Hackett. 1989. *Albion's Seed: Four British Folkways in America*. Oxford: Oxford Univ. Press.

Fischer, John L. 1958. Social influences on the choice of a linguistic variant. *Word* 14:47–56. Reprinted in Dell H. Hymes, *Language in Culture and Society*. New York: Harper and Row, 1964. 483–88.

Forman, E. A., and C. B. Cazden. 1985. Exploring Vygotskian perspectives in education: The cognitive value of peer interaction. In J. V. Wertsch (ed.), *Culture, Communication and Cognition: Vygotskian Perspectives*. New York: Cambridge Univ. Press. 323–47.

Frazer, Timothy C. (ed.). 1993. *"Heartland" English*. Tuscaloosa: Univ. of Alabama Press.

Gordon, Matthew J. 2000. Phonological correlates of ethnic identity: Evidence of Divergence? *American Speech* 755:115–36.

———. 2001. *Small-Town Values and Big-City Vowels: A Study of the Northern Cities Shift in Michigan*. Publication of the American Dialect Society, 84. Durham, NC: Duke Univ. Press.

Graff, David, William Labov, and Wendell Harris. 1986. Testing listeners' reactions to phonological markers. In D. Sankoff (ed.), *Diversity and Diachrony*. Amsterdam and Philadelphia: J. Benjamins. 45–58.

Greenberg, Joseph H. 1959. Language and evolution. In *Evolution and Anthropology: A Centennial Appraisal*. Washington, DC: Anthropological Society of Washington.

Guy, Gregory. 1980. Variation in the group and the individual: The case of final stop deletion. In W. Labov (ed.), *Locating Language in Time and Space*. New York: Academic Press. 1–36.

Haeri, Niloofar. 1996. *The Sociolinguistic Market of Cairo: Gender, Class and Education*. London: Kegan Paul International.

Hazen, Kirk. 2002. Identity and language variation in a rural community. *Language* 78:240–57.

Hershberg, Theodore (ed.). 1981. *Philadelphia: Work, Space, Family and Group Experience in the Nineteenth Century.* New York: Oxford Univ. Press.

Hershberg, Theodore, et al. 1981. A tale of three cities: Blacks, immigrants, and opportunity in Philadelphia, 1850–1880, 1930, 1970. In Hershberg 1981, 461–95.

Holbrook, Stewart H. 1950. *The Yankee Exodus: An Account of Migration from New England.* New York: Macmillan.

Houston, Anne. 1991. A grammatical continuum for (ING). In P. Trudgill and J. K. Chambers (eds.), *Dialects of English: Studies in Grammatical Variation.* London: Longman. 241–57.

Hudley, Anne H. Charity, and Christine Mallinson. 2011. *Understanding English Language Variation in U.S. Schools.* Multicultural Education Series. New York: Teachers College Press.

Jensen, Richard. 1971. *The Winning of the Midwest: Social and Political Conflict, 1888–1896.* Chicago: Univ. of Chicago Press.

Joiner, C. W. 1979. Memorandum Opinion and Order on Civil Action 7-71862. *Martin Luther King Junior Elementary School Children, et al. v. Ann Arbor School District Board.* 473 F. Supp. 1371 (E. D. Mich.).

Kilpinen, Jon. 2009. Course on American Ethnic Geography, Valparaiso Univ., http://www.valpo.edu/geomet/pics/geo200/politics/elazar.gif. (accessed November 8, 2011).

Kniffen, Fred B., and Henry Glassie. 1966. Building in wood in the eastern United States. *Geographic Review* 56:40–66.

Kurath, Hans. 1949. *A Word Geography of the Eastern United States.* Ann Arbor: Univ. of Michigan Press.

Kurath, Hans, and Raven I. McDavid Jr. 1961. *The Pronunciation of English in the Atlantic States.* Ann Arbor: Univ. of Michigan Press.

Labov, William. 1963. The social motivation of a sound change. *Word* 19:273–309. Revised as chap. 1 of Labov, *Sociolinguistic Patterns.* Philadelphia: Univ. of Pennsylvania Press, 1973.

———. 1966a. The effect of social mobility on linguistic behavior. In S. Lieberson (ed.), *Explorations in Sociolinguistics.* Bloomington: Indiana Univ. Press. 186–203.

———. 1966b [2006]. *The Social Stratification of English in New York City.* Washington, DC: Center for Applied Linguistics. 2nd ed., Cambridge: Cambridge Univ. Press, 2006.

———. 1969a. Contraction, deletion, and inherent variability of the English copula. *Language* 45:715–62. Revised as chap. 9 of Labov 1972.

———. 1969b. The logic of non-standard English. In J. Alatis (ed.), *Georgetown Monographs on Languages and Linguistics,* 22. Washington, DC: Georgetown Univ. Press. 1–44.

———. 1971. Academic ignorance and black intelligence. *Atlantic Monthly,* June, 59–67.

————. 1972. *Language in the Inner City*. Philadelphia: Univ. of Pennsylvania Press.

————. 1974. Linguistic change as a form of communcation. In Albert Silverstein (ed.), *Human Communication*. Hillsdale, NJ: Erlbaum. 221–56.

————. 1982a. Competing value systems in the inner-city schools. In P. Gilmore and A. Glatthorn (eds.), *Children In and Out of School*. Washington, DC: Center for Applied Linguistics. 148–71.

————. 1982b. Objectivity and commitment in linguistic science: The case of the Black English trial in Ann Arbor. *Language in Society* 11:165–202.

————. 1984. Field methods of the project on linguistic change and variation. In J. Baugh and J. Sherzer (eds.), *Language in Use*. Englewood Cliffs, NJ: Prentice Hall. 28–53.

————. 1989. The child as linguistic historian. *Language Variation and Change* 1:85–97.

————. 2001. *Principles of Linguistic Change*, vol. 2: *Social Factors*. Oxford: Blackwell.

————. 2007. Transmission and diffusion. *Language* 83:344–87.

————. 2008. Triggering events. In S. Fitzmaurice and D. Minkova (eds.), *Studies in the History of the English Language IV: Empirical and Analytical Advances in the Study of English Language Change*. Berlin: Mouton de Gruyter. 11–54.

————. 2009. A life of learning: Six people I have learned from. American Council of Learned Societies. HTML/audio; mp3. http://www.acls.org/publications/audio/labov/default.aspx?id=4462.

————. 2010a. *Principles of Linguistic Change*, vol. 3: *Cognitive and Cultural Factors*. Oxford: Blackwell.

————. 2010b. Unendangered dialect, endangered people: The case of African American Vernacular English. *Transforming Anthropology* 18:15–27.

Labov, William, S. Ash, M. Baranowski, N. Nagy, M. Ravindranath, and T. Weldon. 2011. Properties of the sociolinguistic monitor. *Journal of Sociolinguistics* 15:431–63.

Labov, William, Sharon Ash, and Charles Boberg. 2006. *Atlas of North American English: Phonology and Sound Change*. Berlin: Mouton de Gruyter.

Labov, William, and Bettina Baker. 2010. What is a reading error? *Applied Psycholinguistics* 31:735–57.

Labov, William, P. Cohen, C. Robins, and J. Lewis. 1968. A study of the nonstandard English of Negro and Puerto Rican Speakers in New York City. Cooperative Research Report 3288. Vols. 1 and 2. Available through the ERIC system, www.eric.ed.gov. Vol. 1: ERIC ED 028423; vol. 2: ERIC ED 028424.

Labov, William, and Wendell A. Harris. 1986. De facto segregation of black and white vernaculars. In D. Sankoff (ed.), *Diversity and Diachrony*. Philadelphia: John Benjamins. 1–24.

Labov, William, Malcah Yaeger, and Richard Steiner. 1972. *A Quantitative Study of Sound Change in Progress*. Philadelphia: U.S. Regional Survey.

Le Baron, Wm., Jr. & Co. 1879. The History of McLean County, Illinois: Portraits of early settlers and prominent men. Chicago: W. Le Baron Jr.

Leaverton, L. 1973. Dialectal readers: Rationale, use and value. In J. L. Laffey and R. Shuy (eds.), *Language Differences: Do They Interfere?* Newark, DE: International Reading Association. 114–26.

Legum, Stanley, Carol Pfaff, G. Tinnie, and M. Nicholas. 1972. *The Speech of Young Black Children in Los Angeles.* Technical Publication, 33. Inglewood, CA: Southwest Regional Laboratory for Educational Research and Development.

LeMoine, Noma. 1999. *English for Your Success; A Language Development Program for African American Children.* Maywood, NJ: Peoples Publishing Group.

Massey, Douglas S., and Nancy A. Denton. 1993. *American Apartheid: Segregation and the Making of the Underclass.* Cambridge, MA: Harvard Univ. Press.

McDavid, Jr., Raven I., and Virginia G. McDavid. 1964. Plurals of nouns of measure in the United States. In Albert H. Marckwardt (ed.), *Studies in Languages and Linguistics in Honor of Charles C. Fries.* Ann Arbor: Univ. of Michigan. 271–301.

McKelvey, Blake. 1949a. A panoramic view of Rochester's history. *Rochester History* 11:1.

———. 1949b. Rochester and the Erie Canal. *Rochester History* 11:3, 4.

Merton, Robert K. 1957. *Social Theory and Social Structure.* Glencoe, IL: Free Press.

Mitchell-Kernan, Claudia. 1969. *Language Behavior in a Black Urban Community.* Monographs of the Language-Behavior Research Laboratory, no. 2. Berkeley: Univ. of California.

Mock, Carol. 1979. The social maturation of pronunciation: A family case study. *The Rural Learner* (Southwest Missouri State Univ.) 1:23–37.

Morain, Thomas J. 1988. *Prairie Grass Roots: An Iowa Small Town in the Early Twentieth Century.* Henry A. Wallace Series on Agricultural History and Rural Studies. Ames: Iowa State Univ. Press.

Myhill, John. 1988. Postvocalic /r/ as an index of integration into the BEV speech community. *American Speech* 63:203–13.

Ogbu, John. 1982. Cultural discontinuities and schooling. *Anthropology and Education Quarterly* 13:290–307.

———. 1987. Opportunity structure, cultural boundaries and literacy. In Judith A. Langer (ed.), *Language, Literacy and Culture: Issues of Society and Schooling.* Norwood, NJ: Ablex. 149–77.

Plichta, Bartłomiej, and Brad Rakerd. 2010. Perceptions of /a/-fronting across two Michigan dialects. In D. R. Preston and N. Niedzielski (eds.), *A Reader in Sociophonetics.* New York: Mouton/De Gruyter, 223–39.

Pope, Jennifer, Miriam Meyerhoff, and D. Robert Ladd. 2007. Forty years of language change on Martha's Vineyard. *Language* 83:615–27.

Power, Richard Lyle. 1953. *Planting Corn Belt Culture: The Impress of the Upland Southerner and Yankee in the Old Northwest.* Indianapolis: Indiana Historical Society.

Raumer, Rudolph von. 1967. Linguistic-historic change and the natural-historical definition of sounds. Trans. Winfred P. Lehmann in Lehmann (ed.), *A Reader in Nineteenth Century Historical Indo-European Linguistics.* Bloomington: Indiana Univ. Press, 1967. 67–86. Originally published in *Zeitschrift für die Osterreichischen Gymnasien* 5 (1856): 355–73.

Reaser, Jeffrey L., and Walt Wolfram. 2006. *Voices of North Carolina: Language and Life from the Atlantic to the Appalachians.* Instructor's manual. Raleigh: North Carolina Language and Life Project.

Rickford, John. 1975. Carrying the new wave into syntax: The case of Black English BIN. In R. Fasold and R. Shuy (eds.), *Analyzing Variation in Language.* Washington, DC: Georgetown Univ. Press. 162–83.

———. 1980. How does DOZ disappear? In Richard Day (ed.), *Issues in English Creoles: Papers from the 1975 Hawaii Conference.* Heidelberg: Julius Groos. 77–96.

———. 1999. *African American Vernacular English: Features and Use, Evolution, and Educational Implications.* Oxford: Blackwell.

Rickford, John R., Arnetha Ball, Renee Blake, Raina Jackson, and Nomi Martin. 1991. Rappin on the copula coffin: Theoretical and methological issues in the analysis of copula variation in African-American Vernacular English. *Language Variation and Change* 3:103–32.

Rickford, John R., and Angela E. Rickford. 1996. Dialect readers revisited. *Linguistics and Education* 7:107–28.

Rickford, John Russell, and Russell John Rickford. 2000. *Spoken Soul: The Story of Black English.* New York: John Wylie.

Roberts, Julia. 1993. The acquisition of variable rules: t,d deletion and -ing production in preschool children. PhD diss., Univ. of Pennsylvania.

———. 1997. Acquisition of variable rules: A study of (-t,d) deletion. *Journal of Child Language* 24:351–72.

Rosenthal, R., and Lenore Jacobson. 1968. *Pygmalion in the Classroom.* New York: Holt, Rinehart and Winston.

Saussure, Ferdinand de. 1959. *Course in General Linguistics.* Ed. C. Bally and A. Sechehaye. Trans. Wade Baskin. New York: Philosophical Library.

Seligman, C. R., G. R. Tucker, and W. E. Lambert. 1972. The effects of speech style and other attributes on teachers' attitudes towards pupils. *Language in Society* 1:131–42.

Shuy, Roger W. 1962. The Northern-Midland dialect boundary in Illinois. *Publications of the American Dialect Society* 38:1–79.

Shuy, Roger, Walt Wolfram, and William K. Riley. 1967. *A Study of Social Dialects in Detroit.* Final Report, Project 6–1347. Washington, DC: Office of Education.

Simpkins, Gary, Grace Holt, and Charlesetta Simpkins. 1977. *Bridge: A Crosscultural Reading Program.* Boston: Houghton-Mifflin.

Simpkins, Gary, and Charlesetta Simpkins. 1981. Cross-cultural approach to curriculum development. In Smitherman 1981, 212–40.

Smitherman, Geneva (ed.). 1981. *Black English and the Education of Black Children and Youth: Proceedings of the National Invitational Symposium on the King Decision*. Detroit: Center for Black Studies, Wayne State Univ.

Snow, Catherine, M. Susan Burns, and Peg Griffin (eds.). 1998. *Preventing Reading Difficulties in Young Children*. Washington, DC: National Academy Press.

Stewart, William A. 1967. Sociolinguistic factors in the history of American Negro dialects. *Florida FL Reporter* 5 (Spring): 2.

———. 1968. Continuity and change in American Negro dialects. *Florida FL Reporter* 6:3–14. Reprinted in Frederick Williams (ed.), *Language and Poverty: Perspectives on a Theme*. Chicago: Markham, 1970. 362–76.

Stokes, Allen W. (ed.). 1974. *Territory*. Stroudsburg, PA: Dowden, Hutchinson and Ross.

Stowe, Harriet Beecher. 1899. *Uncle Tom's Cabin*. Boston: Houghton-Mifflin.

Sturtevant, Edgar. 1947. *An Introduction to Linguistic Science*. New Haven: Yale Univ. Press.

Terry, J. M., R. Hendrick, E. Evangelou, and R. L. Smith. 2010. Variable dialect switching among African American children: Inferences about working memory. *Lingua* 1208:2463–75.

Thomas, Erik R. 2010. A longitudinal analysis of the durability of the Northern/Midland dialect boundary in Ohio. *American Speech* 85:375–430.

Trudgill, Peter. 1974. *The Social Differentiation of English in Norwich*. Cambridge: Cambridge Univ. Press.

———. 1986. *Dialects in Contact*. Oxford: Blackwell.

Vaughn-Cooke, Fay. 1986. Lexical diffusion: Evidence from a decreolizing variety of Black English. In M. Montgomery and G. Bailey (eds.), *Language Variety in the South: Perspectives in Black and White*. University: Univ. of Alabama Press. 111–30.

Weinreich, Uriel, William Labov, and Marvin Herzog. 1968. Empirical foundations for a theory of language change. In W. Lehmann and Y. Malkiel (eds.), *Directions for Historical Linguistics*. Austin: Univ. of Texas Press. 97–195.

Wheeler, Rebecca, and Rachel Swords. 2006. *Code-Switching: Teaching Standard English in Urban Classrooms*. Urbana, IL: National Council of Teachers of English.

Wolfram, Walt. 1969. *A Sociolinguistic Description of Detroit Negro Speech*. Arlington, VA: Center for Applied Linguistics.

———. 2007. Sociolinguistic folklore in the study of African-American English. *Language and Linguistic Compass* 10:749–811.

Wolfram, Walt, and Natalie Schilling-Estes. 2004. Remnant dialects in the coastal United States. In Raymond Hickey (ed.), *The Legacy of Colonial English*. Cambridge: Cambridge Univ. Press. 172–202.

Wolfram, Walt, and Erik Thomas. 2002. *The Development of African American English*. Oxford: Blackwell.

Zelinsky, Wilbur. 1992. *The Cultural Geography of the United States*. Rev. ed. Englewood Cliffs, NJ: Prentice Hall.

Index

AAE (African American English), 40.
See also African American Vernacular English (AAVE)

AAVE. See African American Vernacular English

abolition, 118

absence of elements, 48–54

"Academic Ignorance and Black Intelligence" (Labov), 72

acoustic analysis, 29–30

"acting white," 136

Adams, Mike, 83

additive educational approach to AAVE, 72–73

African American English (AAE), 40. See also African American Vernacular English (AAVE)

African American Vernacular English (AAVE), 7, 38–97; absence of elements in other dialects, 48–54; as additive educational tool, 72–73; Ann Arbor trial on, 74–77; BE DONE, 61–65; and cross-racial contacts, 52; defined, 38–39; and dialect readers, 83–85; divergence from Standard English, 38–67; and Ebonics controversy in Oakland, 77–83; habitual BE, 57–60; HAD as marker of simple past, 55–

57; and Northern Cities Shift, 45, 136; origin of, 45–46; politics of, 68–97; presence of elements not in other dialects, 54–65; and reading achievement gap, 68–71; and Reading Road and Portals to Reading programs, 85–94; regional pronunciation differences, 40–44; remote present perfect BIN, 60–61; and SEEK controversy, 73–74; structure of, 46–48; and students' view of world, 94–97; teaching the possessive to speakers of, 88–91; uniformity of, 39–40

African languages, 45

agricultural terminology, 112

Alabama: AAVE in, 46; voting patterns in, 133

alphabetic principle, 86, 87, 95

American Apartheid (Massey & Denton), 65–66

American Council of Learned Societies, 100

American Federalism: A View from the States (Elazar), 122

Ann Arbor: AAVE trial in, 74–77; Northern Cities Shift in, 28

apical contact, 151n2 (chap. 1)

apostrophe signals, 151n2 (chap. 1)

Appalachia, 26, 88, 114
Ash, Sharon, 25, 26
Atlanta: AAVE in, 39; Reading Road
    program in, 86
Atlantic Monthly publication of "Aca-
    demic Ignorance and Black Intel-
    ligence," 72
Atlas of North American English (Labov,
    Ash & Boberg), 26, 29, 34–35, 36,
    41, 132, 137, 154n10 (chap. 4)
/aw/ diphthong, 104
/ay/ diphthong, 155n2 (chap. 7)

Bailey, Guy, 39, 54, 55, 57, 60
Baltimore, AAVE in, 46
Baptists, 119
Baugh, John, 39, 52, 54, 63
Bayesian Markov chain Monte Carlo
    model, 154n12
BE. *See* habitual BE
BE DONE, 55, 61–65, 153n8
Beecher, Henry Ward, 121
BIN, remote present perfect, 55, 60–61
Birmingham: cross-dialectical com-
    prehension experiments in, 18–19;
    residential segregation in, 65
Black English. *See* African American
    Vernacular English (AAVE)
"Black Nonsense" (Moon), 73
Bloomfield, Leonard, 32–33, 34
Boberg, Charles, 26
Bonfiglio, Thomas, 135, 136
Boston, linguistic divergence in, 35
Bridge: A Cross-Cultural Reading Pro-
    gram, 83–85
broad-a system, 113
broadcast standards: and convergence,
    1, 98; and (ING) variable, 10–12
Brockmann, Dirk, 33, 153n14
Brooklyn College SEEK program, 73–74
Brooklynese, 2, 8, 107
Buffalo: and communication net-

works, 33; and Erie Canal construc-
    tion, 112; Northern Cities Shift in,
    23, 26, 28
"Burned-Over District" (New York), 118
Burnouts, 110

Calculation and Applied Subtests of
    Woodcock-Johnson R-battery, 89
California: AAVE in, 39, 46, 54; Read-
    ing Road program in, 86
California Curriculum Commission,
    39–40; Summary Statement text,
    141–50
California State University–Hayward,
    86
Canada, linguistic divergence in,
    34–35, 155n2 (chap. 6)
"Canadian raising," 155n2 (chap. 6)
careful speech, 10, 14–15, 16
Carwardine, Richard, 119, 124, 134
casual speech: and AAVE, 47; (ING)
    variable in, 10, 13–15, 16
centralization, 100–101, 102
ch digraph, 93
Charleston: linguistic divergence in,
    35; r-less dialect in, 35
Chicago: AAVE in, 46; and communi-
    cation networks, 33; cross-dialec-
    tical comprehension experiments
    in, 18–19, 21–22; linguistic diver-
    gence in, 35; Northern Cities Shift
    in, 17–23, 26, 28; residential segre-
    gation in, 65, 66
Chomsky, Noam, 4
Cincinnati: linguistic divergence in,
    35; residential segregation in, 65
Civil Rights Act of 1964, 133, 134
Cleveland: AAVE in, 39; and commu-
    nication networks, 33; Northern
    Cities Shift in, 28; residential seg-
    regation in, 65
Clinton, Bill, 132

Clinton, DeWitt, 112
coastal communities, 35
Cockney, 35
Columbus: Northern Cities Shift not
    evident in, 29; r-less dialect in, 36
combinatory problems, 86–87
communication networks, 33
conflict management, 94
continuous system, 113
contraction rules, 48, 53
contrastive analysis, 73–74, 78, 91–92,
    93
convergence, 1, 34–37, 98
copula /s/, 88
Cornell University, 82
Cosby, Bill, 80
creole languages, 46
The Crisis (NAACP), 73
Cross, Whitney R., 118
cross-dialectical comprehension,
    18–23, 25, 155n5
cross-racial contacts, 52, 66, 67
Cukor-Avila, Patricia, 39, 54, 57
cultural hearth, 125
culture: and AAVE, 70–71; and Doc-
    trine of First Effective Settlement,
    137–39; and Northern Cities Shift,
    122–25; political, 122–25; and west-
    ward migration, 115, 117
currency movement patterns, 33

Dallas Morning News on AAVE, 76
Darwin, Charles, 4–5
Dayton, Elizabeth, 59, 64, 153n7
decreolization, 46
deletions, 48
Democratic Party: and evangelicals,
    120; and Northern Cities Shift, 8,
    138; and voting patterns, 126–34
Denton, Nancy A., 65–66
Descent of Man (Darwin), 4–5
Detroit: AAVE in, 39, 46, 53–54; and

communication networks, 33;
    Northern Cities Shift in, 23, 26,
    28; residential segregation in, 65
dialect leveling, 6
dialect readers, 83–85
Dictionary of American Regional English
    (Carver), 32, 111
digraphs, 93
dissimilarity index, 154n9 (chap. 4)
divergence, 17–37; acoustic measure-
    ments, 29–30; of black and white
    English, 7, 38–67; as local identity
    marker, 8, 98–108; and Northern
    Cities Shift, 19–25; reasons for,
    32–34; in vocabulary, 17
Dr. Goodword's Language Blog, 1–2
Doctrine of First Effective Settlement,
    125, 137–39
dominance index, 65
double modals, 152n1

EAE (European American English), 42
Ebonics: defined, 80; humor as ag-
    gression toward, 81–83; Oakland
    school board controversy, 77–83;
    Senate hearings on, 85–86. *See
    also* African American Vernacular
    English (AAVE)
Eckert, Penelope, 109–10
-*ed* (past tense), 48, 49
Elazar, Daniel, 122, 125
elections, 126–34
Ellyria, Northern Cities Shift in, 28
Erie Canal, 8, 112–13
European American English (EAE), 42
evangelicalism, 118, 119–20, 134
*Evangelicals and Politics in Antebellum
    America* (Carwardine), 119
evolution of language, 4–5

Fasold, Ralph, 39, 152n7
Fischer, David Hackett, 115, 125

Fischer, John, 9
Flint: and communication networks,
33; Northern Cities Shift in, 28
Ford Foundation, 73, 74
formal speech, 14–15, 16
formants, 29, 31, 103–4
Furman v. Georgia (1972), 122
future perfect BE DONE, 61–63

Gay Head Indians, 101, 135, 155*n1*
(chap. 8)
general raising system, 114
Georgia: AAVE in, 46; voting patterns
in, 133
Glassie, Henry, 114
glide deletion, 155*n2* (chap. 7)
grammar: in AAVE, 40, 65, 79–80;
sources of variation in, 6; stability
of, 17
Grand Rapids, Northern Cities Shift
in, 28
graphemic/phonemic relations, 85
Great Lakes region, 114
Great Migration, 46, 55
Greenberg, Joseph, 5
group vs. individual nature of language, 6–7
Gullah, 46

habitual BE, 55, 57–60, 79–80
HAD as marker of simple past, 55–57
Hawthorne, Larry, 72
Hayes, Rutherford, 133
Hershberg, Theodore, 65
Higgins, Henry, 107
high text-to-self realization, 93
historical linguistics, 4
History of McLean County, Illinois (Le
Baron), 117
Holt, Grace, 83
home language, 75–76, 79
Houghton-Mifflin, 83, 85, 87

Hudley, Anne Charity, 39
hypercorrection, 51

identity. *See* local identity
ideology. *See* political ideology; Yankee
ideology
Illinois: Northern Cities Shift in, 27,
114; voting patterns in, 132. *See also*
Chicago
impressionistic phonetics, 29, 101,
153*n11*
In-Betweens, 110
incrementation, 102
index of dominance, 65
Indiana: Northern Cities Shift in, 29,
114; voting patterns in, 138
individualistic political culture, 124–25
individual vs. group nature of language, 6–7
(ING) variable, 3, 9–16; consensus on,
15–16; defined, 9, 151*n2* (chap. 2);
in New York City, 9–10; origin of,
152*n6* (chap. 2); political use of,
13–15; social perception of, 10–12; in
South Carolina, 12–13
Inland North: and AAVE, 45; and death
penalty, 121–22; divergence in, 34;
Midland divergence from, 31–32;
migration to, 114; Northern Cities
Shift in, 26–29, 30, 136; voting patterns in, 127–30
Inland South, 26
invariant BE, 80
Iowa: death penalty legislation in, 122;
voting patterns in, 132

Jackson, Jesse, 78
Jensen, Richard, 119, 124, 138
Jocks, 110
*Jocks and Burnouts: Social Categories
and Identities in the High School*
(Eckert), 109–10

Johnson, Lyndon, 133
Joiner, Charles, 75
Joliet, Northern Cities Shift in, 28

Kalamazoo, Northern Cities Shift in,
28
Kansas, death penalty legislation in,
122
Kansas City, Northern Cities Shift not
evident in, 29
Kennedy, John F., 133
Kenosha, Northern Cities Shift in, 28
Kensington dialect, 106
Kim, Ron, 155n5
King, Martin Luther, Jr., 80–81
Kniffen, Fred B., 114
Kroch, Anthony, 155n4
Kurath, Hans, 25, 26, 155n1 (chap. 7)

Labov, William, 26, 39, 72
Lambert, W. E., 154n2
language: as individual or group property, 6–7; knowledge of, 2–4; views
of, 1–2, 79
Language Experience method, 77
Le Baron, William, 117
Linguistic Atlas of New England, 100
linguistic research strategies, 4–6
Linguistic Society of America, 79
linguistic tokens, 107–8
linguistic variables, 7, 9–16. See also
specific variables
literacy, 7, 87, 95
liturgicals, 119
local identity, 8, 98–108; and AAVE,
53; in Martha's Vineyard, 98–103;
and Northern Cities Shift, 109–11;
in Philadelphia, 103–7; and social
networks, 107–8
"Logic of Non-standard English, The"
(Labov), 72–73, 92
Long, Russell, 133

long open-o, 20, 152n9
Los Angeles: AAVE in, 39, 46, 54; linguistic divergence in, 35
Louisiana: AAVE in, 46; voting patterns in, 133

Madison, Northern Cities Shift in, 28
Maine: death penalty legislation in,
122; voting patterns in, 132
Martha's Vineyard, 98–103, 135, 155n2
(chap. 6)
Martínez, Maurice, 83
Martin Luther King Elementary School
(Ann Arbor), 74–77
Massey, Douglas S., 65–66
Massillon, Northern Cities Shift in, 28
mass media: and convergence, 1, 98;
and (ING) variable, 10–12
Maynor, Natalie, 55
McDavid, Raven I., 26
McKinney, Ernest, 74
Methodists, 119
Michigan: death penalty legislation in,
122; voting patterns in, 132
middle class, 10, 104, 106
Midland: defined, 152n8; linguistic
divergence in, 35; migration to, 114,
115; North divergence from, 30–32;
and Northern Cities Shift, 25–29;
political culture of, 125; positive
anymore use in, 152n1; voting patterns in, 127, 130
Milwaukee: and communication networks, 33; Northern Cities Shift in,
28; residential segregation in, 65
Minnesota, voting patterns in, 132
miscommunication. See cross-dialectical comprehension
Mississippi: AAVE in, 46; voting patterns in, 133
Mitchell-Kernan, Claudia, 39, 54
Mobile, r-less dialect in, 36

INDEX   169

Montreal French, 154n2
Moon, Henry Lee, 73
Morain, Thomas, 116, 117
moralistic political culture, 124–25

NAACP, 73
nasal system, 113
National Assessment of Educational
    Progress (NAEP), 68
National Institutes of Health (NIH),
    86
National Research Council Committee
    on Preventing Reading Difficulties
    Among Young Children, 85
National Science Foundation (NSF),
    86, 152n3
Nation of Islam, 72, 135
natural selection, 4–5
negative inversion, 152n1
networks of communication, 33
Newark, residential segregation in,
    65, 66
New Deal, 132
New Orleans, AAVE in, 39
newscasting. See broadcast standards
New York (state): death penalty legisla-
    tion in, 122; and Erie Canal con-
    struction, 112–13; Northern Cities
    Shift in, 27–29; voting patterns in,
    132. See also specific cities
New York City: AAVE in, 39, 46; and
    communication networks, 33;
    linguistic divergence in, 35; local
    identity in, 107; Northern Cities
    Shift in, 23; reading achievement
    in, 68–71; residential segregation
    in, 65, 66; r-less dialect in, 35, 42,
    135; (ING) variable in, 9–10
New York Metropolitan Achievement
    Test Reading, 69
-ng spelling, 151n2 (chap. 1)
The North: Midland divergence from,
    30–32; and Northern Cities Shift,

25–29; political culture of, 125;
    pronunciation in, 152n4; voting
    patterns in, 127, 128, 130
North Carolina: local dialects and
    identity in, 35, 155n3 (chap. 6); /r/
    pronunciation in, 42
North Dakota, death penalty legisla-
    tion in, 122
Northern Cities Shift: and AAVE, 45,
    136; acoustic measurements of,
    19–23, 29–30, 99; and cultural
    styles, 122–25; geography of, 7,
    25–29; identifying speakers of,
    23–25; as local identity marker,
    109–11; nonlocal aspects of, 111–12;
    origin and history of, 112–17; politi-
    cal ideology of, 8, 109–34; reasons
    for, 32–34; and religion, 119–21;
    and slavery, 118; sounds of, 19–23,
    29–30, 99; and voting patterns,
    126–34
nouns of measure, 83
NSF (National Science Foundation),
    86, 152n3

Oakland, Ebonics controversy in,
    77–83
Obama, Barack: on education pro-
    grams, 94; (ING) variable use by,
    13–15
Ocracoke, linguistic divergence in, 35,
    155n3 (chap. 6)
Ohio: Northern Cities Shift in, 27; vot-
    ing patterns in, 132
Omaha, Northern Cities Shift not evi-
    dent in, 29
orderly heterogeneity, 10
outward bound nature of language, 6

Palin, Sarah, 14–15
Patrick, Thomas W., 74
Penn Reading Initiative, 86
Pennsylvania: linguistic divergence in,

35; Northern Cities Shift in, 114. *See also specific cities*
ph digraph, 93
Philadelphia: AAVE in, 39, 46, 55, 59–60, 62, 136; black and white pronunciation in, 42–44; cross-dialectical comprehension experiments in, 18–19; Language Experience method in, 77; linguistic divergence in, 35; local identity in, 103–7; and Midland dialect, 155*n*1 (chap. 7); Northern Cities Shift in, 23, 26, 111–12; Reading Road program in, 86; residential segregation in, 65
Philadelphia: Work, Space, Family and Group Experience in the Nineteenth Century (Hershberg), 65
Philadelphia Daily News on AAVE, 76–77
phonemic awareness, 85
phonology: and Northern Cities Shift, 28; sources of variation in, 6
pietists, 119
Pittsburgh: linguistic divergence in, 35; and Midland dialect, 155*n*1 (chap. 7); Northern Cities Shift in, 26
Planting Corn Belt Culture (Power), 116
political ideology: and AAVE, 68–97; of Northern Cities Shift, 8, 109–34; and (ING) variable, 13–15. *See also* Yankee ideology
Poole, Donald, 101
Poole, Everett, 101–2
Portals to Reading program, 85–94; AAVE used in, 91–94; teaching the possessive to speakers of, 88–91
possessive forms, 49, 88–91
Power, Richard Lyle, 116
Prairie Grass Roots (Morain), 116
Presbyterians, 119
presence of elements not in other dialects, 54–65

Principles of Linguistic Change (Labov), 34
progressive verbs, 3
pronunciation: in AAVE, 40–44, 87; (ING) variable, 3, 9–16, 151*n*2 (chap. 2), 152*n*6 (chap. 2); and Northern Cities Shift, 26; in Philadelphia, 42–44; /r/ pronunciation, 35–36, 41–42, 135, 136; short-a, 20, 22, 113–14, 129; short-e, 20, 110, 129; short-o, 20, 22, 29, 152*n*9; short-u, 20, 29, 30–31, 110, 129
Protestantism, 119
Providence, r-less dialect in, 35
Pygmalion effect, 71

Quebecois, 154*n*2

/r/ pronunciation, 35–36, 41–42, 135, 136
race and racial inequality: and Northern Cities Shift, 8; politics of, 135. *See also* African American Vernacular English (AAVE)
Raumer, Rudolph von, 34
reading achievement gap, 7, 50, 52, 68–71
Reading Road program, 85–94
Received Pronunciation, 35
Reed, Carol, 73
reference groups, 103
regional dialects: and AAVE pronunciation differences, 40–44, 64–65; and Northern Cities Shift, 26; persistence of, 36–37. *See also* local identity
regional radio, 98
religion: and AAVE, 72, 135; and Northern Cities Shift, 8, 119–21
remote present perfect BIN, 55, 60–61
Republican Party: and evangelicals, 120, 121; and Northern Cities Shift, 8, 138; and voting patterns, 126–34
residential segregation, 7, 52, 65–67, 68, 135

resultative use of BE DONE, 63–65

Rhode Island, death penalty legislation in, 122

Richmond: AAVE in, 39; r-less dialect in, 35, 36

Rickford, Angela E., 82–83

Rickford, John R., 39, 60, 79, 82–83

Riley, William K., 152*n*7

Rochester: and communication networks, 33; and Erie Canal construction, 112; Northern Cities Shift in, 26, 28

Rockford, Northern Cities Shift in, 28

Roosevelt, Franklin, 35

Rowan, Carl, 76

rural terminology, 112

Rustin, Bayard, 73

Sacramento Bee on Ebonics controversy, 78

St. Louis: AAVE pronunciation in, 41; linguistic divergence in, 35; Northern Cities Shift in, 153*n*13; residential segregation in, 65

Saussure, Ferdinand de, 34

Savannah, r-less dialect in, 35

schools: culture in, 70; segregation of, 68, 138, 154*n*1; violence in, 94, 95

second formant, 29–30, 31, 103–4

Second Great Awakening, 118

SEEK (Search for Education, Elevation and Knowledge) program, 73–74, 78

segregation. *See* residential segregation; schools

Seligman, C. R., 154*n*2

semantic theory, 135

Senate hearings on AAVE, 85–86

sequential BE DONE, 64

sh digraph, 93

short-a, 20, 22, 113–14, 129

short-e, 20, 110, 129

short-o, 20, 22, 29, 152*n*9

short-u, 20, 29, 30–31, 110, 129

shortening rules, 48. *See also* contraction rules

Shuy, Roger, 152*n*7

Simpkins, Charlesetta, 83

Simpkins, Gary, 83

situation comedies, AAVE in, 98

slavery: and AAVE, 46; and Northern Cities Shift, 118

Smith, Ernest, 79

Smitherman, Geneva, 75

Smith Island, 35

social interaction in learning, 154*n*10 (chap. 4)

social learning theory, 154*n*10 (chap. 4)

social motivation of sound changes, 102–8, 139

social networks, 107–8, 110–11

social perceptions of (ING) variable, 10–12

social stratification: and local identity, 104; and (ING) variable, 9, 10, 16

social welfare, 132

sound-to-letter correspondences, 88

South, the: and AAVE, 41, 136; double modals use in, 152*n*1; linguistic divergence in, 35; and Northern Cities Shift, 25–29; political culture of, 125; pronunciation in, 152*n*4; regional dialect fading in, 36; voting patterns in, 130, 132, 133–34

South Carolina: (ING) variable in, 12–13; voting patterns in, 134

Southwestern Regional Laboratory, 39

Specter, Arlen, 85–86

speech community, 10

Spencer Foundation, 86

split system, 113

Standard English and AAVE, 38–67, 78, 87

Stone, Chuck, 76–77, 79–80

Stowe, Harriet Beecher, 120–21

street culture, 50, 70

subject-verb agreement, 51, 52
Summary Statement on African American Vernacular English (Labov et al.), 40; text of, 141–50
superposed dialects, 47
Supreme Court, U.S.: on death penalty, 122; on school segregation, 154*n*1
Swann v. Charlotte-Mecklenburg Board of Education (1971), 154*n*1
Syracuse: and communication networks, 33; and Erie Canal construction, 112; Northern Cities Shift in, 28

television programs, AAVE in, 98
temperance, 118
Texas, AAVE in, 39, 46, 54, 57, 60
Texas South region, 26
text-to-self realization, 93
Thematic Apperception Test, 9
Thomas, Erik, 32
Times-Picayune on Ebonics controversy, 78
Toledo, Northern Cities Shift in, 28
traditionalistic political culture, 124–25
Tucker, G. R., 154*n*2

UD criterion, 29–30
Uncle Tom's Cabin (Stowe), 120–21
universal grammar, 4
University of North Carolina, 89
University of North Carolina–Wilmington, 83
University of Pennsylvania, 86, 152*n*3
Upland Southerners, 115
upper class, 10, 106, 155*n*4
Utica: and communication networks, 33; and Erie Canal construction, 112; Northern Cities Shift in, 28

Vassar, 82
velar contact, 151*n*2 (chap. 1)
verbal -*s*, 49–52, 83, 88, 90

Vermont, voting patterns in, 132
vernacular, 47, 52
Vespignani, Alessandro, 153*n*14
violence in schools, 94, 95
vocabulary: divergence in, 6, 17; and Northern Cities Shift, 25, 28, 111
voting patterns, 126–34
Voting Rights Act of 1965, 134
vowel systems: acoustic analysis of, 29–30; and Northern Cities Shift, 17–23, 99, 136; patterns of, 100; in Philadelphia, 42–43
Vygotsky, Lev, 154*n*10 (chap. 4)

Wald, Benji, 23
Walker's Dictionary, 35
Walsh, Sean, 78
Washington, D.C., AAVE in, 39
West, the: AAVE in, 39; linguistic divergence in, 35
West African languages, 45
West Virginia, death penalty legislation in, 122
Wilkins, Roy, 73–74
Williams, Robert, 79, 86
Williams, Walter B., 79
Winning of the Midwest, The (Jensen), 119
Wisconsin: death penalty legislation in, 122; Northern Cities Shift in, 27; voting patterns in, 132
Wolfram, Walt, 39, 40, 42, 53, 152*n*7, 155*n*3 (chap. 6)
Woodcock-Johnson R-battery, 89
working class, 10, 104

Yankee ideology: cultural style of, 117, 124–25, 134; and death penalty, 121–22; and religion, 119–21; and slavery, 118

Zelinsky, Wilbur, 137
zero tolerance policy, 95

Page-Barbour and Richard Lectures (in print)

Edmund S. Morgan
The Meaning of Independence: John Adams, George Washington, and Thomas Jefferson

Johannes Fabian
Moments of Freedom: Anthropology and Popular Culture

Ian Hacking
Mad Travelers: Reflections on the Reality of Transient Mental Illnesses

Harvie Ferguson
Modernity and Subjectivity: Body, Soul, Spirit

Stephen Mulhall
The Conversation of Humanity

Freeman J. Dyson
A Many-Colored Glass: Reflections on the Place of Life in the Universe

Maurice Godelier
In and Out of the West: Reconstructing Anthropology
Translated by Nora Scott

Richard J. Smith
Fathoming the Cosmos and Ordering the World: The "Yijing" ("I Ching," or "Classic of Changes") and Its Evolution in China

Martin Jay
The Virtues of Mendacity: On Lying in Politics

Jean-Luc Marion
The Reason of the Gift
Translated by Stephen E. Lewis

Robert B. Pippin
Fatalism in American Film Noir: Some Cinematic Philosophy

Lyndal Roper, *The Witch in the Western Imagination*

William Labov
Dialect Diversity in America: The Politics of Language Change